·STONE·
CARVING

- for the -
HOME & GARDEN

·STONE· CARVING

- for the -
HOME & GARDEN

STEVE BISCO

THE GUILD OF MASTER CRAFTSMAN PUBLICATIONS

First published 2012 by
Guild of Master Craftsman Publications Ltd
Castle Place, 166 High Street, Lewes,
East Sussex BN7 1XU

ISBN 978-1-86108-844-4

Publisher Jonathan Bailey
Production Manager Jim Bulley
Managing Editor Gerrie Purcell
Senior Project Editor Virginia Brehaut
Copy Editor Nicola Hodgson
Managing Art Editor Gilda Pacitti
Design Ali Walper

All photographs by the author except the following:
Page 22: stone supplier's yard and big saw photographed by the author with the kind permission
of Collins & Curtis Masonry Ltd., Ipswich, England. Page 25 (bottom right): by kind permission of
Axminster Tool Centre, Axminster, England. Page 32 (bottom, far left and bottom, middle left) and
page 33 (bottom left) iStockphoto/Thinkstock

Set in Charlemagne, Berkeley Oldstyle and Interstate
Colour origination by GMC Reprographics
Printed and bound in China by Hing Yip Printing Co. Ltd

CONTENTS

Introduction

WELCOME TO THIS BOOK ON STONE carving for the home and garden. It may well be the first book on stone carving that you have seen. How do I know that? Because, when I decided to take up stone carving after 25 years of carving wood, I found that books on stone carving were almost non-existent. Having already produced a book on woodcarving (*Twenty Decorative Carving Projects in Period Styles*), I soon concluded that if I wanted a book on stone carving then I would have to write it myself – so I did. Here it is, and I hope it will help you follow the hobby of stone carving without the trouble of writing your own book.

Stone carving is a very ancient art. When I say it's not rocket science, I mean that as a virtue. Technologically, it couldn't be simpler. You take a piece of rock, millions of years old, dug out from the very fabric of our planet and, using the very simplest of tools, you chip out all the bits you don't want until you are left with a shape that is the product of your own skill and imagination. Humankind has been doing this for many millennia, and the results of these endeavours survive for hundreds and thousands of years.

Stone carving is quite underdeveloped as a hobby. Historically, it has always been practised by architectural stonemasons who are taught under long apprenticeships to decorate cathedrals and grand buildings, and by sculptors, who are taught in art studios to create statues of the human figure.

We (if I may speak for you as well as myself) represent a third group – the hobby stone carver, producing a mix of decorative and sculptural objects on a smaller scale to satisfy our creative instincts and to decorate our homes and gardens. We, generally, are not in a position to undertake a long apprenticeship or a full-time course of study, nor do we generally have the resources to tackle large and heavy blocks of stone.

The 18 projects in this book are designed to be accessible to the average hobby carver in the average home. They are arranged into four groups that will allow you to develop your skills from raw beginner, if that is your starting point, to accomplished hobby stone carver. I hope the projects will give you as much pleasure as they have given me.

ABOUT THIS BOOK

This book is for anyone who has ever thought about carving stone as a hobby, whether or not you have previous carving experience either in stone or wood. It takes you through the basics of working in stone, and leads you through 18 decorative and sculptural carving projects to develop your skills as you create impressive stone objects for your home and garden. If you are already a woodcarver, you will have no trouble adapting to stone. If you have no carving experience, this book tells you what you need to know to work your way up from a zero starting point.

The projects are based mainly on the period styles of carved ornament found in historic buildings and ancient ruins. They will be of particular interest to anyone who likes to visit historic buildings, and wants to create that feel at home. Four of these projects have previously been published in *Woodcarving* magazine, while the rest have been created specially for this book.

Each project includes:
- A pattern you can copy to full size
- Step-by-step photos
- Instructions so you can follow the process

The projects start with quite simple pieces and work steadily upwards to more challenging ones, each building on skills learned in the previous projects. But, unlike many learning courses, there are no boring exercises. You learn as a by-product of creating attractive decorative objects for your home and garden – and you go as far and as fast as you choose.

CARVING FOR THE HOME AND GARDEN

Most people who carve as a hobby, myself included, live in average-size houses with average-size gardens. Few of us have the space or resources to build, say, a triumphal arch, an equestrian statue or a Bernini fountain. We set our sights on more modest goals. The projects in this book are designed to be of a manageable scale for a hobby carver and suitable for the average home. They have, in many cases, been scaled down from period originals or been specially designed to capture the spirit of a period or style in a compact piece.

Stone, for all practical purposes, is weatherproof. If, like me, you are also a woodcarver, you will know how quickly you can fill up your house with woodcarvings. Carving in stone provides carvers with an opportunity to expand beyond the confines of the house.

Some of the smaller items in this book are suitable for indoor display, especially in a conservatory where the sun's glare will not fade them; in a bathroom, where steam and water will not bother them, or on a fire hearth where they will not be troubled by heat. All of them can be displayed in the garden, even on the smallest patio. The 'Rocky ruins' in particular (projects 4 to 10) can be scattered around on rockeries and among plants. Instead of moulded concrete urns and statues from the local garden centre, your garden can be filled with original stone carvings created with your own hands.

Decorative and sculptural stone carvings, indoors or out, can really lift the spirits, especially when you have made them yourself. You can add to your collection piece by piece – until you eventually have to move to a bigger house!

LEARNING STEP BY STEP

We all learn in different ways. Some people learn easily from written instructions; some people prefer to be shown one to one by a tutor. This book tries to strike a balance. Obviously, I can't be there beside you as you work, but I can provide you with pictures of what you will see at each stage of a project, and describe as clearly as I can what you need to do next.

Looking at a photo of a finished stone carving that appears to be beyond your level of experience can be daunting. It is less daunting when you see the process of making that carving broken down into a number of individual steps.

You then begin to see not only how to tackle the job, but that each one of those steps is achievable. Some of them may stretch you beyond your present level of experience, but that is part of the pleasure of developing your skills. The point is that you don't have to progress in giant leaps. Each new step builds on something you will have tackled in an earlier project, like walking up a flight of stairs one by one instead of trying to jump from floor to floor.

With the step-by-step approach you will soon be tackling carvings you never dreamed you could take on, and developing skills you never knew were within you.

USING THE PATTERNS

Each of the projects has a pattern you can enlarge to create a full-size drawing. In some cases, the pattern is traced onto the stone; in others, it is used to make templates, and in some projects the drawing is just for guidance and taking measurements from.

Each pattern is set out with gridlines that equate to 1in (25mm) squares when blown up to actual size. It is up to you what size you make your carving, but if you want to make it the same size as my original and relate it to the measurements quoted in the instructions, you should enlarge the drawing so the gridlines are 1in (25mm) apart.

You can enlarge the pattern with a photocopier, scan it into your computer with a scanner, or photograph the page with a digital camera and print it out in sections on your computer. If you use the camera method, don't put the camera too close to the page – it will create

a fish-eye lens effect, causing the sides of the drawing to bulge outwards and distorting the proportions. Place the camera further back, get it square on to the page, and use the zoom to focus in on the page. When you look at the image on the computer, check there is no significant distortion in the gridlines – they should be straight, parallel and square.

You can also work in the old-fashioned way, which is more flexible and often easier. Just mark out a large sheet of paper with 1in (25mm) gridlines – the same number as on the drawing. Mark reference letters and numbers in the squares along the top and sides of the book page and your sheet. Now just draw whatever lines you see in each square onto your sheet in the same square. Tidy up the lines at the end, and you will have a full-size drawing. Using this method, you can easily scale a drawing up or down to any size you want just by adjusting the width of your gridlines.

STONE-CARVING TOOLS

The tools used for stone carving have changed little over the centuries. Because the craft is so old, the tools required were developed a very long time ago, and there has been no real need to change them. The only significant difference is in the hardness of the steel. Today, we have carbon-steel and tungsten-tipped tools, which hold a sharp cutting edge much better than anything our ancestors could make. If you are a woodcarver, and especially if you are a woodturner, you will be used to paying out quite large sums of money on tools. By contrast, you can acquire tools for stone carving for quite a modest sum. You only need about a dozen tools, and these are usually much cheaper than their woodworking equivalents.

Mallets

Stone carving is a fairly gentle process, requiring only gentle taps on the chisel or gouge from a small 'dummy' mallet. However, for dressing and roughing out a stone with a point and bolster before carving, you will need a weightier club (or 'lump') hammer. Some carvers prefer a wooden mallet, which gives a bigger hitting area for the same weight. I instinctively shy away from hitting metal with wood, but that is a personal preference.

Repeatedly swinging a heavy hammer is hard on the wrist, elbow and arm muscles, so choose the lightest hammer that will do the job effectively. I find that a 1½lb (655g) dummy mallet for detail carving and a 2½lb (1175g) club hammer for roughing out gives the right balance between impact and effort.

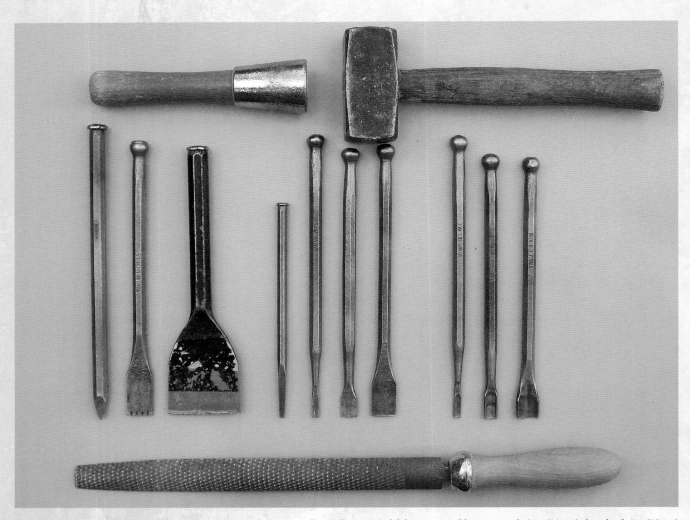

Stone-carving tools (from top, then left to right): 1½lb (655g) dummy mallet, 2½lb (1175g) club hammer, marble point/punch, ¾in (20mm) claw chisel, 2in (50mm) bolster/pitcher, ³⁄₁₆in (4mm) chisel, ¼in (6mm) chisel, ½in (13mm) chisel, ¾in (20mm) chisel, ¼in (6mm) gouge, ½in (13mm) gouge, ¾in (20mm) gouge, stone rasp. (NB: Metric sizes are actual size – imperial conversions are made to the nearest ¹⁄₁₆in.)

Roughing-out tools

The first stage when starting a carving is usually roughing out, and sometimes 'dressing' the stone (see page 27). This is mainly done using three basic tools: a point tool, a claw chisel and a bolster.

A **point tool** is used to break out the bulk of the unwanted stone. There are two different versions: the marble point and the stone punch. There is little difference between them other than that the stone punch tends to be a bit heavier. The marble point is not just for marble, and a light marble point will meet your needs as a hobby stone carver working with limestone. The point tool is largely non-directional; it will chip out a chunk of stone of indeterminate shape and size along shock lines from the point of impact, so it needs to be used carefully when you get near to the required surface.

The **claw chisel** is used to remove stone in a more controlled manner down to the required surface. The points along the cutting edge allow it to break up the surface more easily than a flat chisel. It leaves a surface a bit like a ploughed field in miniature. You can buy claw chisel shafts with replaceable claws, which is how they are generally sold for the building trade for working concrete and coarser silicate stones that have a severe blunting effect. For carving limestone, however, a normal claw chisel with a fixed head, as illustrated here, is perfectly suitable as the blunting effect is minimal.

The **bolster** is used as a roughing-out tool to flatten and square off a surface, and as a finishing tool to smooth it level. A pitcher is a similar tool for stone-working, but tends to be more expensive than a regular bolster that you can buy from a hardware store. Bolsters (also called 'boasters' by stonemasons) come in a selection of widths; a 2in (50mm) width is the most useful.

A point tool.

A claw chisel.

A bolster.

Chisels

Most of a stone carver's work is done with just a few flat chisels. This may seem surprising to woodcarvers, but it results from the inherent difference between stone and wood. Wood has a longitudinal grain and, if you can't approach a cut from the right angle and direction, the wood will split. Wood, therefore, requires a wide range of tools.

Stone is made up of tiny round or angular grains. This allows the stone carver much more flexibility in the angle and direction of cut, so more can be achieved from a small number of tools. The four chisels in the main tools picture, ranging in width from 3/16in (4mm) to 3/4in (20mm), are all you need. They can be used to shape any flat or convex surface.

You will see tools sold as 'carbon steel' and 'tungsten-tipped'. Carbon-steel tools are suitable for the projects in this book, which are mainly in limestone. Tungsten-tipped tools are more expensive, and are more suitable if you intend to do a lot of carving in granite or marble. However, tungsten tips are more likely to break off than carbon-steel tips.

Chisel shafts come in several sizes and thicknesses. I find a shaft about 9in (230mm) long x 3/8in (10mm) thick is the most comfortable to use. Chisels also vary at the hammer end. Some are flat-headed, and some are round-headed (known as 'mallet-headed'). I prefer mallet-headed chisels and gouges; used with a round dummy, they are less sensitive to the angle at which they are hit. Flat heads are better on roughing-out tools where a heavy impact from a club hammer is needed.

A flat chisel.

Gouges

Gouges are very similar to chisels, but the cutting edge is curved into a shallow U-shape. They are mainly used to shape concave surfaces, but can also be used 'upside down' to finish off narrow convex details. They are less effective than chisels at removing stone, so they are mostly employed as finishing tools after the main shaping has been done by the chisels.

As with chisels, you will only need to use a small range of sizes. The three illustrated in the main tools picture will be sufficient for these projects.

A gouge.

Rasps and rifflers

Most of the work of the stone carver is done by the impact tools described above, but sometimes a gentler approach is needed. Rasps, and their smaller cousins, rifflers, can be used to shape the stone by a process of abrasion. This can be useful along fragile edges, and where a weakness in the rock makes it inadvisable to risk the 'shock' of an impact tool. These tools work best on fairly soft limestone and will tend to slide off really hard stone.

Rasps can be useful for rounding over larger convex, and to a lesser extent concave, surfaces that need a smooth curve. Rifflers, being smaller and available in a variety of shapes, are useful for getting into awkward places for undercutting edges. Rifflers tend to be more expensive than chisels and gouges, and I have not used them in the projects in this book.

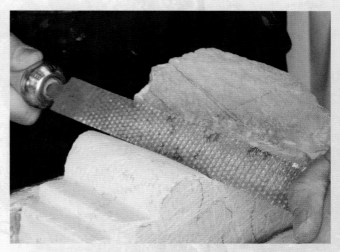
A stone rasp.

Saws

Surprisingly, saws have been used on stone for a long time. Like the rasp, a saw can be useful in cases where you want to remove a section of stone without the shock of an impact tool. Generally, using a saw is no quicker or easier for removing stone than using the roughing-out tools described above, but it can be useful in certain cases. I have used the stone saw on several of the projects in this book where I thought an impact tool might fracture the stone.

You can buy a stone or concrete saw quite cheaply from a building tools supplier. It looks much the same as a carpenter's saw, but has bigger teeth and is made of hardened steel. For finer work, you can buy tile-cutting blades for a junior hacksaw, which are effective on limestone.

A stone/concrete saw.

Power tools

How you feel about power tools depends to some extent on your personal inclinations. Some people automatically reach for a power tool to do every job, whereas others (like me) prefer the quietness and control of hand tools. I tend to use power tools less and less in carving, as I find they rarely save much time and rarely produce as good a result. They also tend to be a bit 'fierce' and can wreck a job in seconds. My advice is to master hand tools first before you reach for a power tool. It will make you a better carver and you will be better able to judge when to use a power tool.

The power tool most used in stonework is an angle grinder with a stone-cutting disc. Modern masons use these extensively, and they have a place in the stone-carver's armoury for cutting out large sections of surplus stone quickly. Like the stone saw, they can be useful where an impact tool may fracture the stone. However, angle grinders must be used carefully. Like most power tools, they are noisy, dusty and violent. They can quickly remove more stone than you intended, and remove parts of your body you certainly hadn't intended, so take great care with them (see page 24).

A rotary multi-tool is a smaller and less violent power tool that can be used to good effect for fine finishing of detail on a carving, especially small hollows. They were not used in traditional stone carving for the simple reason that they were not available, but modern sculptors often use them, and they are particularly effective on marble.

Powered pneumatic chisels and gouges are available to replicate the range of hand chisels and gouges described previously. They come with a power unit and interchangeable heads, and are like a mini-version of the pneumatic drills used by road-workers. They tend to be used by production stone workers whose time is money, and are a fairly expensive option for the hobby carver. Vibrating tools are quite noisy and can cause nerve damage if used for long periods, so bear this in mind. I used vibrating chisels in woodcarving for a while, but soon went back to my hand tools because they were almost as quick and much more fun. The choice is yours, but my advice is to master hand tools first before you think about powering up.

Angle grinder with a stone-cutting disc.

A rotary multi-tool.

Sharpening chisels and gouges

Limestone has the very endearing habit of sharpening your chisels and gouges for you as you work. The abrasive nature of the stone, and the angle at which you apply the tool, has the same effect as using a carborundum sharpening stone (something woodcarvers can only dream of). Marble, granite and sandstone are not so obliging in this way, so you will need to sharpen your tools from time to time (and always when you first buy them).

The method of sharpening is much the same as for a woodworking chisel. Use a flat carborundum stone, with some oil applied, and push the cutting edge of the chisel along it at an angle of about 30 degrees to the horizontal. Repeat the process a few times until the cutting edge, and particularly the points at each end of it, are nice and sharp.

To sharpen a gouge, you need to 'roll' it from side to side as you move it along the sharpening stone. You also need a special curved-edge stone for the concave side of the gouge.

If a tool is very blunt, you can grind it on a grinding wheel, but making it too hot can ruin the tempering of the steel. Use a water-cooled wheel running at a fairly slow speed, and hold the cutting edge at about 30 degrees to the face of the wheel. Grinding on a wheel will, of course, gradually shorten your chisel, so only do it when necessary.

Stone chisels do not have the finger-cutting razor edge of a wood chisel, but you will soon notice the difference between a sharp and a blunt chisel when you come to use it. The end points should dig into the stone easily and cut a good clean edge.

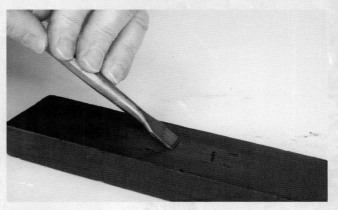
Flat carborundum stone.

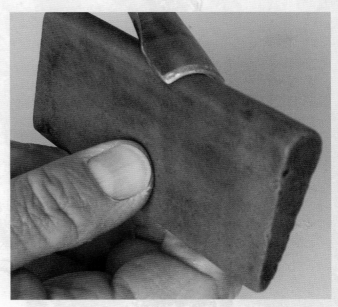
Curved-edge carborundum stone.

Water-cooled grinding wheel.

Buying stone tools

Although you can buy a small range of masonry chisels, bolsters and concrete saws from a good building tools supplier, you will need to get most of your stone-carving tools from a more specialist source. You probably won't find one in your local area, but they do exist. The Internet and mail order are a blessing for those of us who have minority interests. Search the Internet for 'stone carving tools' and you will certainly find a supplier who can offer a wide range of tools and dispatch them directly to your door.

You can also search under 'stonemasonry tools', but this will bring up the industrial end of the market as well, so keep looking until you find the types of tools illustrated in this book. Also check your local directory, craft magazines and art stores. Companies that supply materials for artists and sculptors are the most likely place to find stone-carving tools.

Workbench

If you have a strong bench of a suitable height in your workshop or garage, this should be adequate for many of the projects in this book. However, it needs to be of a comfortable working height, and must allow you to access the carving from many angles without continually having to turn the stone around. It must also allow access to get a heavy stone onto the bench using lifting equipment (see page 25).

Stone is usually heavy enough to stay still while you are working on it, but for smaller pieces you may need to fix wooden strips to the bench, or use a carpenter's bench vice to hold the work still.

Traditionally, a stone carver works on a stout free-standing bench called a banker (an old stonemasonry term presumably derived from the French 'banc', for bench). You can buy a banker from the same source as your chisels and gouges, but they are expensive and it is not difficult to make your own. A free-standing banker allows you to work inside or out, and move freely around the work.

Building a banker

1 Construct a strong solid table with a top about 21in (535mm) square. Use 3in (75mm)-square timbers for the legs, and 3 x 2in (75 x 50mm) timbers for the braces and top. Fix it together with 3in (75mm) screws – they will withstand the weight of the stone and the shock of heavy hammering. Make sure that each leg is braced by horizontal 'stretchers' and diagonal braces so there is no movement in any direction. Make sure the table stands level on a flat surface.

2 Because the table must bear heavy weights, the bearers for the tabletop must bear directly onto the leg timbers, and not just onto screws. Cut a half-joint in the 3in (75mm) leg and fix the 2in (50mm) bearer onto it.

3 I recommend having a separate 'pallet' top for the table. It allows you to adjust the working height by several inches, depending on the height of the carving you are working on. It also allows you to use the pallet to move the stone around more easily with a hoist, a scissor-lift trolley or rollers (see page 25). The pallet top is made of $^3/_4$in (20mm) exterior ply top and bottom, with 2in (50mm) timbers between. Use screws to secure it to the table when in use.

4 The ideal height for your banker depends on your own height. To avoid fatigue, you should be able to work on a carving without bending over. If you want to use a scissor-lift trolley to move stone onto the banker you also need to consider the maximum lift height. I have made the base table 29in (740mm) high to accommodate this. The pallet top, which can be rolled off the scissor lift or lifted up with a hoist with the stone on it, adds another $3^1/_2$in (90mm). This fits me, at 5ft 8in (173cm) tall, but you will need to find the height that suits you best.

STONE - THE MATERIAL

Stone is one of the most abundant materials on the planet, which is probably why humankind has used it for so many purposes. There are much easier materials to work with, but stone seems to be ingrained in the human psyche. Perhaps overcoming the many challenges it presents is part of the attraction. Before we can become stone carvers, if only on an amateur basis, we need to learn how to obtain and handle this hard and heavy substance.

Types of stone

Stone falls into three main groups: igneous, sedimentary and metamorphic rocks.

IGNEOUS ROCKS

Igneous rocks are silicates formed from the molten magma of the Earth's core where it cools on or near the Earth's surface. They generally do not make good carving stone. The best-known, and most abundant, of the igneous rocks is **granite**. Most people are familiar with the grey or greenish granular appearance of granite, usually as polished worktops or 'sets' in cobbled roads. Granite is very hard, very resistant to weathering, and difficult to work with hand tools. Despite this, it is sometimes used by sculptors, but is not for the faint-hearted. It has a significant blunting effect on tools, and only really achieves its decorative potential if highly polished.

SEDIMENTARY ROCKS

Sedimentary rocks are a testament to the very great age of our planet. They are rocks that have been formed, as the name suggests, from the accumulation of sediment in seas and lakes over a very long period, followed by an unimaginably long period of compression. They fall mainly into two groups: sandstones and limestones.

Sandstones are silicates built up from deposits of sand, compressed for hundreds of millions of years into solid rock. Some are very fine-grained, whereas others, such as millstone grit, are coarse-grained. They are deposited in layers that can have a tendency to de-laminate when exposed to frost or heat. The colour of sandstone is often affected by the presence of iron salts, which can leach out to create brown streaks down a wall.

Sandstone is widely used for building and carving, often being the most readily available rock in an area. Many sandstones, however, do not weather well. The fine silica grains are held together by even finer natural cements, some of which are easily dissolved or broken down by water, salt, frost and wind-blown particles. This is often clearly visible on buildings in sandstone areas.

Carvers using sandstone for their carvings must choose rock that is known to have a good resistance to de-lamination and erosion. They must also consider the blunting effect sandstone has on tools and the risk of respiratory illnesses from silica dust (see page 24).

A piece of granite.

A piece of sandstone.

Limestones are formed from deposits of calcium carbonate, made up either directly of coral reefs and the shells and bones of prehistoric marine creatures, or from lime dissolved or eroded from such fossil deposits and reformed as new limestone. Life on Earth is so very old, and very abundant, that this process has been repeated many times, producing vast regions of limestone. Limestone is the stuff of dinosaur legend – the 'Jurassic Park' of stone – the source of the fossils that first made scientists realize the immense age of the planet and the long process of evolution. Expect to meet many 300-million-year-old creatures when using limestone.

Limestone is the preferred rock for stone carving, and the projects in this book feature limestone carving almost exclusively. It is quite easy to work, it doesn't blunt your tools, it is fairly resistant to weathering, the dust is not toxic, and it is generally quite attractive in appearance. As you progress through this book you will become more familiar with the properties of limestone.

Limestones, like all sedimentary rocks, vary considerably in hardness, colour and quality because each bed is the product of the individual circumstances under which it was laid down hundreds of millions of years ago. Some areas are renowned for top-quality limestone, such as Caen in Normandy, France, and Portland in southern England.

METAMORPHIC ROCKS

Metamorphic rocks are sedimentary rocks whose form has been changed by heat and pressure, resulting from movement or volcanic activity in the Earth's crust. The two best-known examples are slate and marble.

Slate – formed from clay deposits – is of very little interest to most stone carvers, although it is sometimes used for incised lettering.

Marble – formed from limestone – is widely used by sculptors, although it requires skill and hard work to produce a good result. It is much harder than limestone, but not as hard as granite. It has a crystalline structure that is easily 'bruised' if the impact from the tool causes the surrounding crystals to separate. Marble is often coloured with mineral veins, and pure white marble, such as Carrara marble from Italy, is highly valued for sculpture. To achieve its full decorative effect, marble needs careful polishing with abrasives.

A softer form of metamorphic limestone is **alabaster**. It was much used in the past for fine sculptures, being very easy to work. Alabaster is not easily available in Britain, as most quarries are now worked out, but Utah and Colorado alabaster are available in the USA. If you can obtain some, cherish it and use it for something special. However, it must be kept dry and indoors, as it is easily dissolved by water.

A piece of limestone.

A piece of marble.

Sourcing stone

For most carving projects, you need to obtain supplies of a good limestone. Buying limestone for carving can be a problem if you don't live near a good quarry or stone supplier. You may need to do some research on the Internet, in your local directory, or by asking around. Monumental masons (gravestone makers) may be able to point you to a suitable supplier. Architectural masonry suppliers are a better source, but bear in mind that masonry is a term also used for bricks and paving blocks, so don't be led off-course.

ARCHITECTURAL STONE SUPPLIERS

Architectural stone suppliers are the best source of quality limestone. A stone supplier's yard is a stone carver's adventure playground. They have saws cutting huge blocks to any size, and if you are lucky they will sell you the off-cuts from these blocks, large enough for hobby projects, at reasonable prices. Try to build up a good relationship with your nearest supplier – it will work to your advantage.

KITCHEN WORKTOP SUPPLIERS

Firms that supply stone worktops for kitchens can be a useful source for thin slabs such as those used in projects 1, 2 and 3. Ask if they have any small off-cuts, and tailor your project to the sizes they have available as it becomes expensive if they have to cut a piece to size.

An industrial stone saw.

A stone supplier's yard.

GARDEN CENTRES

Garden centres are the best source for the rockery stone used in the Rocky Ruins section, projects 4 to 10. Look for the wire bins of fairly soft, creamy limestone (sold in the UK as Cotswold Stone) or the nearest equivalent where you live. It is a cheap way to buy stone, and although it usually carves quite well, expect the quality to be variable. Fossils, soft spots and blast cracks will occur in inconvenient places, but for a Rocky Ruin this just adds to the challenge for the carver and the individuality of the carving.

Rockery stone on sale at a garden centre.

RECLAMATION YARDS

Architectural salvage, or reclamation, yards can be a good source of second-hand building stone. The only problem is that the stone will have hardened considerably from exposure to air and water over the years so will be much harder to work than newly quarried stone.

QUARRIES

If you live anywhere near a good limestone quarry you should have no problem getting supplies of stone. It may be in rough form, so you will have to work it down into blocks by hand (such rock will be quite cheap). Most quarries, however, will be able to supply cut blocks of stone.

Quarrying is a skilled trade. Sedimentary rocks occur in layers, sometimes less than 12in (300mm) thick, called the natural bed. The natural bed may have been tilted or even folded up like a carpet by geological movement. The stone may have shakes (cracks), clay pockets, holes eroded by water, soft spots, colour streaks, and fossils placed inconveniently. It may also, depending on how the quarry has been worked, have random fractures created by high-explosive blasting. These problems are most likely to be found in rough rocks (such as the Rocky Ruins projects in this book), but are less likely to be found in a quarry worked for building and carving stone.

The way a stone is cut in relation to the natural bed (the bedding plane) is important to stonemasons and architectural stone carvers, as it affects the stone's ability to withstand the pressure of the stones above and resist weathering. It is of less importance to the hobby stone carver, but generally speaking, stone should be carved with the natural bed horizontal to the base. When you order cut stone you should state the length, breadth and height, with the height always the last measurement. This tells the stone supplier how the stone should be aligned to the bedding plane.

HANDLING STONE SAFELY

With all crafts, it is important to be aware of the potential risks and take steps to minimize them.

Eye protection

Always wear eye protection when chiselling stone, and full-face protection when using an angle grinder or powered stone-cutter.

Dealing with dust

The dust from granite, sandstone and other silicates can cause silicosis, a serious respiratory illness. Limestone dust is generally considered harmless as it is calcium-based, but repeated exposure to any dust can cause allergies and respiratory problems, so it is best to avoid breathing dust as far as possible.

- Work outdoors whenever feasible to reduce exposure to dust.
- In the workshop, regularly use a workshop vacuum cleaner to remove dust from the carving and surrounding area as you work. This not only helps maintain a healthy environment, but also helps you see the carving more clearly as you work.
- Always wear a dust mask when working with sandstone, granite and other silicates, and for all stone when using an angle grinder or powered stone-cutter.

Lifting and moving stone

Stone is very heavy. A cubic foot, or 300mm metric cube, weighs around 150lb (68kg). Before you buy a piece of stone for a project, or attempt to move a piece, calculate its approximate weight.

- **To calculate a rough weight by *inches*, multiply width x depth x height x 0.087. This will give the rough weight in *pounds*.**
- **To calculate a rough weight by *centimetres*, multiply width x depth x height x 0.0025. This will give the rough weight in *kilograms*.**

Generally speaking, the best way to lift and move stone is NOT by using your back. Use rollers to move stone from one flat surface to another without lifting it. Rolling pins or lengths of metal tube make good rollers. When stone is on the ground, a sack barrow is the best way to move it around without having to lift it.

Removing dust with a workshop vacuum cleaner.

Moving stone on a sack barrow.

Lifting stone with a hoist

The traditional way of lifting stone onto a banker is with a hoist. The best and most economical form of hoist for the hobby carver is the hydraulic engine hoist. Using an engine hoist, one person can lift a heavy block very easily. The hoist will have a stated maximum safe working load, which you must compare to the calculated weight of your stone.

The stone will need to be suspended from the hoist by webbing lifting straps, securely tied under and around the stone so it cannot fall out. Stone will fall much more quickly than you can move, and can cause serious injury if it hits you, so don't ever let this happen. Proper lifting straps also have a stated safe working load. Using the pallet top for the banker described on page 18 makes it easier to secure and remove the webbing straps without having to manhandle the stone. Make sure you get no part of your body underneath the stone while it is suspended, and stand to one side while hoisting.

SAFE WORKING LOAD

When using a hoist you must know the safe working load for every part of the lifting equipment. This includes the hoist, the lifting straps and any hooks, shackles or fixings used to suspend the straps. The equipment is only as strong as its weakest part. If the equipment doesn't come with a stated safe working load, get advice from a qualified person.

Using a scissor-lift table

A scissor-lift table is another option for moving and lifting stone on a flat workshop floor. It is suitable for taking blocks from a vehicle and on to the banker provided the floor surface is smooth. They have a maximum lift height, which must be taken into account for your workbench or banker (see page 18) and a maximum safe working load, which is generally less than an engine hoist. To move stone on and off a scissor-lift table, use rollers as described above.

Lifting stone with an engine hoist.

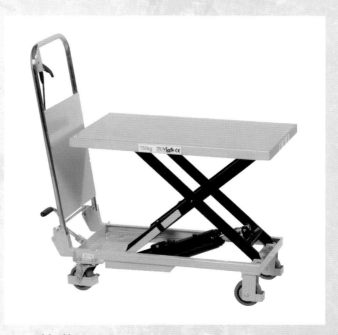

A scissor-lift table.

THE BASICS OF STONE CARVING

The best way to learn stone carving is by practice, which is why this book contains 18 projects for you to work through. Before we embark on the projects, it is worth learning a few of the basics of stonemasonry and stone carving. Architectural stonemasons serve a long apprenticeship to master all the skills needed to create stone buildings, but fortunately the aspiring hobby stone carver needs only to reach a reasonable standard in a few of these skills.

Holding and using the chisel

The first thing to learn is how to hold a chisel or gouge in a comfortable grip, and to make it do what you want.

1 Take the chisel in the opposite hand to the one that you normally write with. Lay it across your hand with the 'mallet' end lying over your thumb.

2 Now close your fingers over the tool, with your thumb still 'outside' the shank. It may feel a bit odd at first, as it is different from how you hold a wood chisel, but you will soon find it becomes second nature. It is less tiring on the hand and gives better control.

3 Take the mallet or 'dummy' in the hand you write with. Place the cutting edge of the chisel, or one of the points at the end of the cutting edge, against the stone at an angle of around 30 degrees (or a bit steeper if the stone is very hard). Hold the dummy or mallet much nearer the head than you would for woodworking – even holding the head of the dummy itself for gentle taps.

4 Tap the chisel along gently with the dummy. You should produce small grains and powder rather than chips and chunks. This is the basic process you will follow for all detail carving.

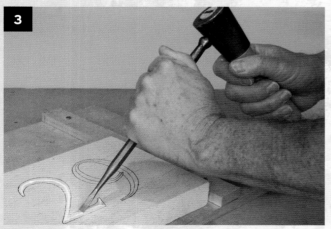

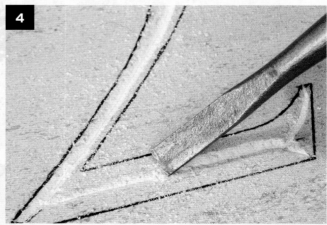

'Dressing' a stone

To a working mason, 'dressing' a stone to six dead-flat surfaces with perfect square corners and sharp straight edges (or 'arrises') to an accuracy within $\frac{1}{20}$in (1mm) is the most basic of the stonemason's skills. The hobby carver, fortunately, rarely needs to achieve these standards, but you will find it useful (and good practice) to be able to work a stone to a flat surface. This is important if you need to put a flat and stable base on a sculpture made from rough stone, and for tracing patterns onto a 'Rocky Ruin'.

1 The first stage in dressing a rough rock is to remove the bulk of unwanted stone with a point or punch. This needs a heavier mallet, and in the early stages you will be knocking off large chips of stone. As you get nearer the required surface, take out smaller chips. Work in parallel lines to create 'furrows', then repeat the process at right angles.

2 Level off a strip around the edges of the block with a claw chisel or bolster. Now check that the opposite edges are on the same plane using the 'two rulers' trick. Sight up two rulers on opposite edges to see whether they are exactly parallel and level. Repeat the process at right angles on the other pair of edges.

3 When the edges are level in all directions without any twisting, cut across from corner to corner with the claw chisel, using a steel rule to check that each strip is dead flat and level with the edges.

4 Now remove the high points between the flat surfaces and check again with the steel rule. Use a bolster to work the surface dead flat and smooth. Work lengthways, crossways and diagonally, moving the bolster in short strokes, so that all high spots are removed (and pity the apprentice mason who would have had to work the face all over again if he had created any pitted areas!).

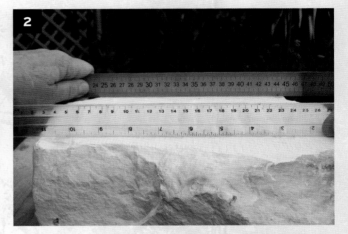

Types of stone carving

Stone carvings fall into four main categories, all of which are represented within this book. They are: incised carving, relief carving, decorative carving in the round, and figurative or figure sculpture.

INCISED CARVING

Incised carving is where the pattern is cut below the surface. The background is the surface of the stone (usually, but not always, flat) and every part of the pattern is below the background. It is the simplest (and the oldest) form of carving and is the best starting point for a beginner. Projects 1, 3 and 4 are based on incised carving.

RELIEF CARVING

'Relief' is a strange word, and in this context has no connection with a feeling of relief (which you may or may not get from carving!). It is used in the topographical sense, as with a 'relief map' of mountains. A relief carving is one where the pattern is raised above the background, to a greater or lesser degree. Although I say 'raised', carving is a 'subtractive' method of shaping, so what actually happens is that the background is cut away to leave the pattern standing above it. The pattern can then be shaped into the desired form.

Relief carving is mainly associated with decorative carving on buildings. It is used to decorate panels, mouldings, string-courses and just about any surface of any shape that needs embellishment. The level of relief can be low, medium or high. As the level of relief gets higher, the pattern is usually undercut around the edges to make it appear detached from the background. Relief carving can range from very simple to very difficult depending on the type of pattern and depth of relief. Projects 2, 4, 5, 6, 9 and 10 are low-, medium- and high-relief carvings on panels and mouldings.

High-relief carving.

Incised carving.

Low-relief carving.

Decorative carving in the round.

DECORATIVE CARVING IN THE ROUND

'Decorative' carving is the term for any form of carving used to decorate a surface or object, as distinct from 'figurative' carving (see below). Carving in the round produces free-standing objects as opposed to the embellishment of surfaces in incised or relief carving. Carving a free-standing object presents different challenges. The object must have structural integrity so it doesn't fall over or fall apart. It also requires the carver to think and work in three dimensions. Many home and garden ornaments fall into this category, and projects 11 to 14 are four such ornaments.

FIGURE SCULPTURE

Figurative carving – the carving of human or animal figures – is often referred to as 'sculpture' and its products as 'statuary'. Its supreme form was achieved by sculptors such as Michelangelo and Canova, but we will not be aiming that high. This book contains four free-standing figurative projects (projects 15 to 18). One is based on the human head and three on other mammals. Two of the Rocky Ruins projects are also human forms in high relief.

Figure carvings are the most difficult to master, both technically and artistically. Like any free-standing carving, they must stand up and not break up. But they have an additional challenge – the slightest deviation in carving the features of a face, especially a human one, can completely alter the expression and general appearance. If you can master figure carving, you can create any number of ornaments for your home and garden.

Figure sculpture.

Stages in a carving

Methods of tackling a carving vary according to the scale and complexity of each piece, but most carving projects are broken down into the following stages: preparing drawings and templates, roughing out the stone to shape, carving the detail, and finishing off.

DRAWINGS AND TEMPLATES

Since ancient times, stonemasons have used full-size drawings and templates to make every stone fit into its place in an arch, vault or wall. Although fitting stones together is less important for carvers, every project should start with a full-size drawing of the carving. This allows you to work through any problems on paper rather than on the stone, and gives you a pattern to measure against or trace onto the stone. Every project in this book has a pattern you can enlarge to full size, giving you the essential dimensions of the piece.

For some carvings, a cardboard or MDF template, prepared from the drawing, is used. Drawing round a template onto the stone is often easier than tracing on the pattern, and you can keep checking against the template as you work.

Tracing a pattern.

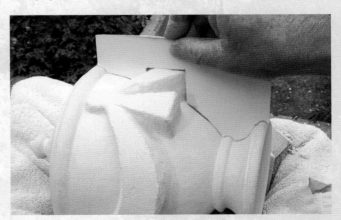

Using a template.

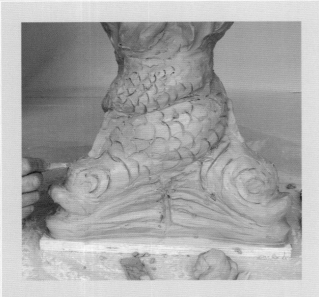

MAKING A MODEL, OR MAQUETTE

In a more complex free-standing carving, it is often helpful to make a model, or maquette, to work out the three-dimensional shape in soft and malleable clay rather than hard stone. The maquette can be full-size, if practical, or made to a smaller scale.

You can buy modelling clay from most art stores. Mould it in your hands to build up the shape of the object, then use small spatulas (either home-made or bought from an art store) to form the detail elements. Some structures may need to have wooden supports to stop the clay from collapsing.

This process is the opposite to carving; you are adding material instead of taking it away. You can keep remoulding the clay until you are happy with the shape. Instead of working from a flat drawing, you now have a three-dimensional model to refer to as you carve. You will need to keep the model covered in plastic wrap or a damp cloth as it will shrink and crumble if it dries out.

ROUGHING OUT

Roughing out is the process of reducing a rough rock or a squared block to the general shape we need for our carving. It basically involves removing all the stone we don't want so we can carve the bit we do want.

The roughing-out stage is often the least interesting, most time-consuming and most physically tiring part of a carving project – but it is an essential part of the process. If you were just to start the detail carving without first having formed the basic shape, you would waste a lot of time correcting the detail and the result would almost certainly be unsatisfactory. Roughing out is a bit like having to do your chores before you can go out to play. You want to get on with the more interesting detail carving, but first you have to work down to the carving surface. You have to learn to love it and curb your impatience to get on with the 'real carving'.

Much of the roughing out will be done using bigger and heavier tools such as the point/punch and the claw chisel. In some cases you will also resort to saws, rasps and even an angle grinder. It can be messy and dusty, so always try and work outside if possible.

CARVING THE DETAIL

This is the stage of the carving that everything else leads up to – the bit where you add the details that give the carving its distinct appearance. In a decorative carving, this will be where you carve the finished form of the decorative elements. In a figure carving, it will be where you carve the face and other physical features that define the person or creature you are trying to create.

Roughing out to remove surplus stone.

Detail carving generally requires the smaller tools in the toolkit – the chisels and gouges. The gouges carve out the concave surfaces, and the chisels form the convex surfaces and the sharp edges. The points on the ends of the cutting edge of the chisel give a very sharp line to delineate any feature.

There is another tool that is essential to detail carving but is often overlooked – the pencil. Before you cut away stone that you cannot put back, draw in the feature with a hard pencil to make sure it looks right. It is easier to rub away a pencil mark than to reshape a bad cut in the stone

FINISHING

Many carvings are finished as soon as the detail carving is completed, without any further work needed. But some need a bit more work to finish them off. This may consist of putting a moulding around the base, or a chamfer around the edge. Some carvings, such as sculptures of the human face, may need a fine 'polished' finish (see box).

Most carvings need at least a thorough wash-down with a hose to remove all the dust from the surface and crevices. Then, of course, there is the question of where to put it.

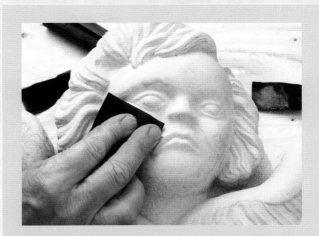

POLISHING STONE

Polishing a stone carving is done mainly by using fine abrasives of the 'wet and dry' variety. These are graded by the size of the grit; the higher the number, the finer the grit. Start with a grit size of 120 to 180, and work up through 240, 400 and 600 until you have a smooth satin finish. Keep the surface wet as you work, and hose off the paste and slurry that forms.

For a higher gloss on an indoor object, you can follow the abrasives with marble polish, which you can buy from a hardware store.

Carving the detail on a decorative carving.

Carving the detail on a figure carving.

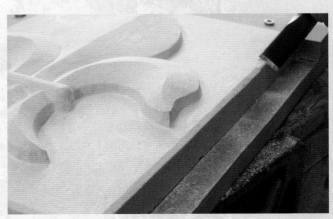

Finishing touches – putting a chamfer along an edge.

PERIODS AND STYLES OF STONE CARVING

A complete history and stylistic analysis of stone carving would fill several books much larger than this one. However, if you intend to carve stone as a hobby it helps to have some understanding of the historic periods and styles of architecture and art that have influenced stone carving over the centuries – at least those of the Western world (the East would fill another book).

Prehistoric carving (700,000–3000 BC)

People have been carving patterns into stone for around 700,000 years. Because they lacked metal tools, most of their carving consisted of incised patterns created by painstaking abrasion with stone tools. As time went on, the patterns became more sophisticated, developing into the Neolithic (New Stone Age) rock art that abounds in caves and tombs throughout the world. Gradually, stone carving expanded into small human and animal figures mainly associated with religion and the afterlife.

Ancient Egyptian (3000 BC–300 AD)

Around 5,000 years ago, the inhabitants of Egypt, who until then had been producing the primitive carvings described above, started to expand their repertoire. Most of us are familiar with the megalithic statues of the Nile valley, with

their stylized beards and striped *nemes* headcloths, and the low-relief hieroglyphic panels decorating the tombs of pharaohs. Egyptian art revolved around religion and the afterlife. As well as the gigantic monuments in human form erected in worship of their god-pharaohs, they also worshipped animal forms such as cats, dogs, bees and serpents, which represented various forms of reincarnation.

Egyptian carving can be considered the first 'modern' style in the sense that it was produced using methods similar to those we use today. It can also appear modern because of its influence on the French 'Empire' style of the early 19th century (following Napoleon's invasion of Egypt in 1798) and the Art Deco style of the 1930s inspired by the discovery of Tutankhamun's tomb in 1922.

Project 15 (page 136) and project 16 (page 144) are based on Ancient Egyptian originals.

Classical Greek and Roman (500 BC–400 AD)

If stone carving came of age in the Egyptian period, it arguably reached its peak in the Classical period around 2,000 years ago. The statuary of the ancient Greeks and

Prehistoric carving.

Abu Simbel, Egypt.

Roman acanthus swirl panel with decorated mouldings, The Forum, Rome.

Roman Ionic capital, The Forum, Rome.

Romans has perhaps been equalled in recent times, but never surpassed. Their magnificent statues of gods such as Hercules, goddesses such as Venus and statesmen such as the Caesars define this period as a high point in the history of figure sculpture. Unfortunately, we tend to see these works in a museum environment with arms and noses missing, but there is no mistaking the quality of the carving, usually in the difficult medium of marble.

The standard and complexity of the decorative carving on their buildings demonstrates how advanced these people were compared to the 'barbarians' of surrounding lands. Greek and Roman architecture was dominated by columns. The tops of these columns were headed by capitals; these developed over a period of time into the 'orders' that became so important to the neoclassical *cognoscenti* of more recent times – Doric, Ionic, Corinthian and Composite, each one more complex than its predecessors.

Surface decoration abounded with acanthus swirls, fruit and flower festoons, processional friezes and many other Classical forms. These would be used to decorate pediments over doors, windows and grand entrances, as well as string-courses and other architectural features. The most famous of the processional friezes adorned the Parthenon in Athens, but now resides in the British Museum and is better known as the 'Elgin Marbles' (see project 9).

A typical feature of the Greek and Roman style is the huge vases decorated with swags of fruit and flowers, rams' heads, drapery and egg-and-dart mouldings. These required an enormous amount of work for the stonemasons who had the job of hollowing them.

Our familiarity with Classical styles is due not just to the historic originals, but to the Classical 'revivals' of more recent times, discussed later.

Project 5 (page 64) is based on an ancient Roman original, and project 9 (page 90) is ancient Greek based on part of the Parthenon frieze. Other Classical projects relate more to the 'revival' periods discussed later.

Medieval period (1000–1500 AD)

The period that followed the collapse of the Roman Empire in the 5th century is generally known as the Dark Ages (450–1000 AD). We can pass quickly over it except to mention the Celtic style that is familiar to us in the jewellery of the Celts and Saxons, and the stone Celtic crosses with their intricate knotwork. The next significant development in the history of stone carving after the demise of the Roman Empire was the Romanesque style, which spread across Charlemagne's Holy Roman Empire in the 9th century. This style was taken up enthusiastically in Norman churches and cathedrals, its key features being thick solid walls and semicircular arches.

Roman columns, The Forum, Rome.

Gothic nave, Rouen, France.

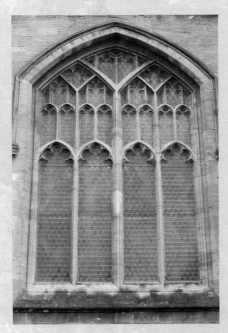
Gothic tracery window, Sherborne, England.

Gothic west front, Rouen, France.

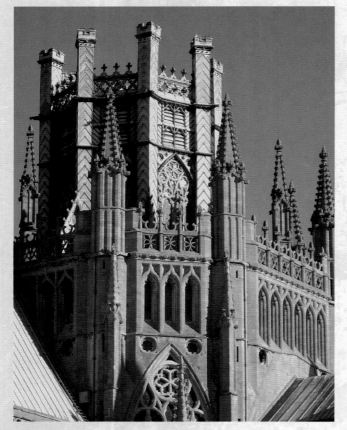

Gothic pinnacles, Ely, England.

The most significant development by far was the Gothic style that started around 1150. Gothic must count as another of the high points in the history of stone carving, and stonemasonry in general. It not only gave us its distinctive gargoyles, crockets, flying buttresses, lierne vaults and tracery, but it was also a great technological advance in the use of stone. A framework of thin stone columns enabled the roof to soar upwards without thick supporting walls, allowing the outer skin to be filled with enormous windows and delicate stone tracery.

The Gothic skyline was a forest of towers and crocketed pinnacles, but the greatest glory was reserved for the west door of every cathedral. With the 'choir' or 'apse' located at the east end, in the direction of Jerusalem, the great west door was the point of entry for the congregation, who must have been awed and humbled by the majesty of the building towering over them.

The Middle Ages also brought another major development in carved decoration: heraldry. Its shields, supporters, crests, mottos and heraldic emblems have been carved in stone from the 12th century to the present day, surviving through all the Gothic and Classical Revival styles.

Project 4 (page 58) is in the Norman Romanesque style. Projects 7 (page 76) , 8 (page 82) and 17 (page 152) are in the Gothic style. Project 2 (page 44) is a heraldic fleur-de-lys emblem.

From the Renaissance to Victorian Revivals (1500–1900 AD)

The next great leap forward was also a step back in time – the revival of the Classical Greek and Roman style after a slumber of a thousand years. This started around 1500 in Italy and was known as the Renaissance (literally 'rebirth'). It gradually spread across Europe, mutating Classical elements into Gothic buildings before eventually emerging as a true reflection of Classical Rome. Classical style went through several variations before returning to its roots. The ornate Baroque style of the 17th century was defined by the depth, richness and exuberance of its stone carving. Many of the great churches of Rome, and Bernini's famous fountains, were built in this period. The Rococo style, with its wild and frivolous acanthus swirls and elaborate gilded plasterwork, dominated the first half of the 18th century, before giving way to a more refined and restrained Georgian Neoclassicism in the second half.

Neoclassical portico, Hudson Valley, New York, USA.

By the 19th century, the Greek Revival had brought Classical styles back to their ancient roots with a pureness and correctness that derided the frivolity of the previous century. This 'masculine' form of Neoclassicism was especially popular in the USA and was used widely in public buildings and grand houses.

Gothic was pushed into the background for a while, but rose up again to dominate the 19th century with the Victorian Gothic Revival. Gothic enthusiasts like A.W.N. Pugin (1812–1852) recreated a pure Medieval Gothic in the many new churches built in this period, but also adapted Gothic to the modern demands of large public buildings and private homes. The Gothic Revival was embraced enthusiastically in America, Europe and throughout the British Empire.

Project 6 (page 70) is from the Renaissance period. Project 10 (page 96) is from a Baroque original, and projects 14 (page 126) and 18 (page 160) are in the Baroque style. Project 12 (page 110) is in the Neoclassical style.

Modern times (1900–present day)

The 20th century started off quite promisingly with the striking stylized forms of Art Nouveau before Art Deco started us on the slippery slope towards Modernism and abstract art. Carved decoration has declined in the last hundred years, but in the long history of stone carving a hundred years is just a coffee break, so who knows what will develop in the next 700,000 years!

The Baroque Trevi Fountain, Rome.

Victorian Gothic, Houses of Parliament, London, UK.

Art Nouveau facade, Riga, Latvia.

PART 1

Getting started with flat panels

HAVING COVERED THE BASICS OF stone carving such as the tools, materials, methods and the historical background, we can now move from theory to practice.

These three projects, two of them incised carving and the other in low relief, are designed to get you started with the process of removing stone in a controlled manner. Incised carving is a good starting point as you can get straight into detail carving without the sometimes laborious work of roughing out. The amount of stone you have to remove is small, and the process of removing it is gentle. What it teaches you above all else is control, and that is the key to successful stone carving.

I promised at the start of this book that there would be no boring exercises, so I hope that by tackling these projects you will make something that gives you pleasure as well as practice. When you take up a hobby, its primary purpose is enjoyment, and anything you learn in the process should add to that enjoyment. Everything you absorb in

these projects pushes you further up the learning curve and gives you a foundation for the next one. I hope you will also be proud to display your creations.

The first project produces a stone number plaque, but if your house doesn't have a number you may like to substitute this with letters such as initials or a name.

The second project, a heraldic fleur-de-lys, gives you a first taste of low-relief carving, in which you cut away the background to leave the pattern raised. You also practise levelling off the background to a smooth surface.

The third project, a Victorian-style ivy pattern, tackles a more elaborate incised carving and gives you practice in working with a harder stone than the first two projects: marble, as opposed to limestone.

You should be able to get the small limestone panels from a stone supplier or a producer of kitchen worktops, and the marble slab from a garden centre.

HOUSE NUMBER PLAQUE

*The phrase 'every home should have one' could be applied to many things,
but to function in a civilized world every home needs an address. For most of us,
this will be a number to identify the position of our house within a street.*

In the long history of stone carving, house numbers are a relatively recent invention, apparently starting in Paris in 1512 but only catching on slowly. I have several original books dating from the 17th century where the booksellers' addresses in London read like a list of directions, like one William Freeman whose premises in 1685 could be found 'over against the Devil Tavern by Temple Bar in Fleet Street.'

Most countries have had house-numbering systems in their cities for a couple of centuries, but this practice is less common in rural areas. I live in a large village where house numbering was introduced only in my lifetime. My house now bears the number 29 and is consequently much easier to locate than when it just had a name.

The size and shape of your plaque will depend on how many digits there are in your house number. The USA probably presents the biggest challenge to carvers of house numbers. Many cities, and even whole states, are numbered in a grid of 'blocks', with the first one or two digits in a four- or five-digit number being the number of the block. If this applies to you, a longer slab will be needed than for my modest two digits.

Making a number plaque for your house (or name plaque if it has no number) is a good starter project for carving stone. It involves carving incised numbers into a small limestone slab with very simple tools. Done neatly, with a classic typeface, it will lend dignity to your home and acquaint you with the basic technique of removing stone in a controlled manner. Done badly, however, it will say 'a caveman lives here', so try to avoid this effect.

For this project, I suggest you try to obtain small off-cuts of limestone from firms that make kitchen worktops from stone. You can pick these up quite cheaply, and they are suitable for small practice projects. The piece I have used here cost me just a small donation to the mason's refreshment fund.

TOOLS
1½lb (655g) dummy mallet • ¼in (6mm) chisel
• ½in (13mm) chisel

MATERIALS
Limestone panel about 1in (25mm) thick x 6in (150mm) high. The width should be about 1, 1½ or 2 x the height depending on how many digits you have in your house number (1, 2-3 or 4).

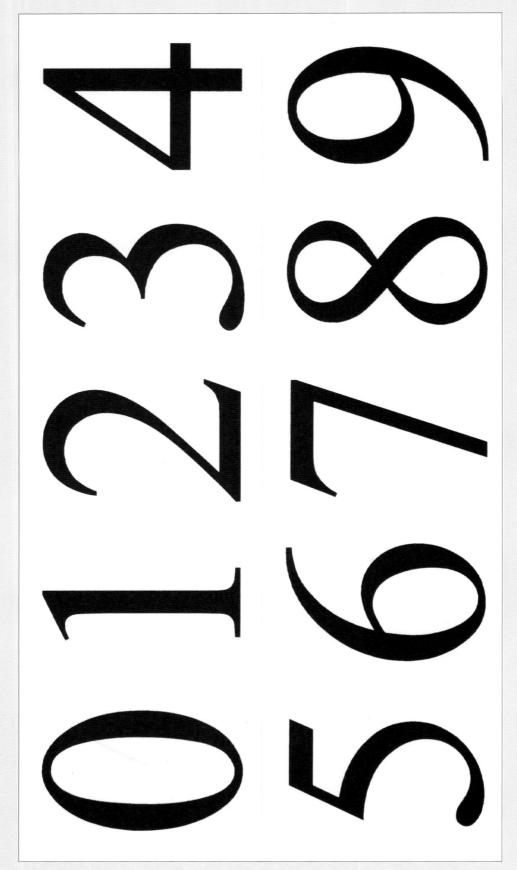

Enlarge relevant numbers to the required size.

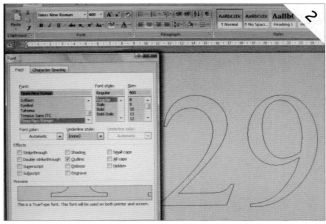

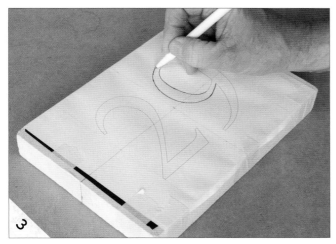

PREPARATIONS

1 Get a piece of limestone about 1in (25mm) thick and about 6in (150mm) high. The width should be about 1, 1½ or 2 times the height depending on how many digits are in your house number (1, 2–3 or 4). For my two digits, this plaque is 9in (230mm) wide. The only tools you will need are a ¼in (6mm) masonry chisel, a ½in (13mm) masonry chisel and a small mallet or mason's dummy. Choose a piece of stone with a good smooth finish and a pleasing appearance, as its surface will be a key feature on this carving.

2 Make a full-size drawing of your house number. You can either copy from the numbers shown on the facing page or, if you have a computer, you can set up a customized print. Type your number onto a Word document and set the typeface and font size to suit your plaque. Times New Roman is a good font for incised lettering. Key in a very large font size setting, using about 100 points for every 1in (25mm) in height. I have set mine to 400 points for a height of nearly 4in (100mm). Call up the font menu and select 'outline'. This gives you just the outline of the number, which is easier to trace from.

3 Carefully position the number centrally (horizontally and vertically) on the plaque. Mark the centrelines on the drawing and on the edge of the stone (attach some masking tape to the stone and draw onto that to avoid leaving dirty marks). Place some carbon paper under the drawing, tape the drawing securely in place so it doesn't move, then trace the outline of the numbers carefully onto the stone. Use a ruler on the straight lines.

4 Measure and mark the centreline of each number, taking note of where the centrelines meet at the junctions. We are now ready to carve. Stone is surprisingly fragile at the edges and corners, so take care not to damage these. Keep the bench free of chippings as you work (use a brush or a heavy-duty vacuum cleaner), as these are enough to crumble an edge that is placed upon them. There is no 'give' in stone.

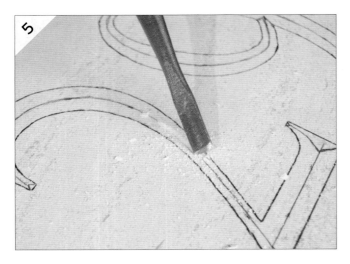

CARVING THE NUMBERS

5 Attach some edge strips on your workbench to stop the work sliding about, and put on some safety glasses as a precaution against stray stone chips. Pick up your ¼in (6mm) chisel and dummy, using the mason's grip (see page 26). Place the point at the lower end of the cutting edge on the centreline of a number and, with the chisel at a low angle and the cutting edge slanting at 45 degrees, chip along the line very gently. If the chisel skids off without making any impression on the stone, increase the angle of entry and tap a bit harder. Make short rapid taps – not big whacks. You should score a shallow groove in the stone, creating powder and grit as you go, not big chunks of stone.

6 Repeat this process with the chisel cutting edge slanted to the opposite side, opening out the V as you go. Go very gently, especially in the narrower parts, so you don't crumble away stone outside the edges of the letter.

7 Keep repeating this process, working along the centrelines of each letter. Make the sides of the V about 45 degrees. This means the V gets deeper as it gets wider. When the side of the V becomes wider than the ¼in (6mm) chisel, switch to the ½in (13mm) chisel.

8 At the junctions of the centrelines, you have to judge how the V of each section will interface with the adjoining section. This depends on the angle at which the sections join, and the width of the respective parts. Each join will create internal or external mitres in the Vs – make these nice and sharp. The serifs (the little curled points at some ends) need particular care. Carve inwards at corners and serifs, as a crumbled corner will spoil the appearance of the letter.

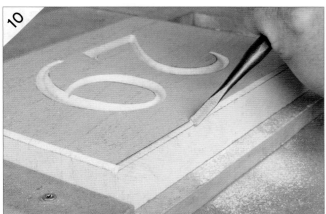

FINISHING

9 Finish the edges carefully up to the guidelines and make sure the centres of the Vs are crisp and in the right place. Be aware that the guidelines may distract your eye from the actual cut edge of the letter, so check carefully. You can leave the letters with a 'tooled' finish showing the chisel lines, or you can smooth them off by sliding the chisel along like a plane. This helps straighten the lines.

10 Draw a line along the front and sides of the block 1/16in (2mm) in from the top outer edge. Carefully cut a chamfer along these edges at 45 degrees. This creates a tidier edge without any crumbly bits.

11 Wash the stone clean and rub it with a dry cloth to bring up a slight polish. To fix it on your house you can either set it into the brickwork – a 6 x 9in (150 x 230mm) panel is the size of two bricks – or you can drill two holes in the back and hang it on nails fixed in the wall. You could also screw it to the wall by drilling screw holes right through the block and using decorative screw heads, but be aware that the metal may corrode and stain the stone.

FLEUR-DE-LYS PANEL

The fleur-de-lys, with its distinctive three leaves or petals bound in the middle by a cross-band, is a decorative device much used in heraldry since the early Middle Ages. It was the key feature of the arms of the kings of France, and of England from 1340 to 1801, when English monarchs claimed to be the rightful heirs to the French throne. The fleur-de-lys is very similar to the Prince of Wales' feathers – except that the latter device is more 'feathery'. Given the impact that the Middle Ages and heraldry had on the development of traditional decorative stone carving, the fleur-de-lys makes an appropriate subject for an aspiring stone carver to practise.

This project builds on the experience gained in project 1 by taking you to the next step – carving in low relief. Whereas incised carving removes the material that makes up the shape you want to create, low-relief carving does the opposite – it removes the material *around* the shape you want to create, leaving it standing above the surface. You then carve the raised pattern to give it a three-dimensional shape (although in a very shallow form) that appears to sit on the surface of the background you have created.

Like Project 1, this project also uses a small slab of limestone about 6 x 9 x 1¼in thick (150 x 230 x 30mm), which you can probably obtain as an off-cut from a firm specializing in making kitchen worktops. You will be removing about ½in (13mm) depth of stone, so the 1¼in (30mm) thickness is the minimum – any less than this would run the risk of breaking the slab.

Tooling up for this job couldn't be simpler or cheaper; the whole project can be carved with a ½in (13mm) mason's chisel. However, if you have set yourself up with a full kit of tools, you can usefully employ several more of them.

This project will give you a first taste of creating a dead-flat surface with your own tools – a skill you will develop further as you progress through the projects.

TOOLS

1½lb (655g) dummy mallet
- ½in (13mm) chisel

MATERIALS

Limestone panel about 6 x 9 x 1¼in
(150 x 230 x 30mm)

Scale drawing on a 1in (25mm) grid. Enlarge drawing to the required size (see page 10).

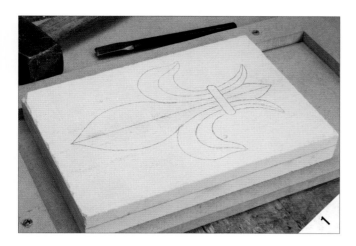

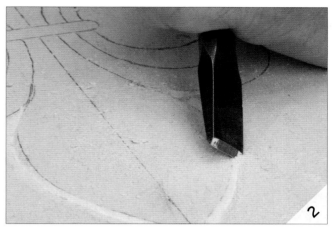

PREPARATIONS

1 Start with a piece of limestone about 6 x 9 x 1¼in (150 x 230 x 30mm) and a full-size copy of the drawing. Trace the pattern onto the stone panel using carbon paper, and draw a line all the way around the edge ½in (13mm) from the front face. With a small piece like this you need to attach some edge strips to the bench to stop the work sliding about (a heavy block would stay put on its own). You also need to work on a dead-flat surface, such as a sheet of MDF, as any unevenness could cause the panel to break.

GROUNDING OUT THE PATTERN

2 Place the point of the chisel on the outside edge of the pattern line at an angle of about 45 degrees, and make a shallow cut around the pattern. Give the chisel short sharp taps with the hammer to move it along steadily but gently, about ¹⁄₁₆–⅛in (2–3mm) at a time. Don't whack it hard or you will just take chips out of the bits you want to keep. Aim to produce powder and grit, not chunks.

3 Open out the V by cutting from both sides, getting to a progressively steeper angle on the pattern edge as you work down. Clear away the dust as you work, either with a brush or preferably with a heavy-duty vacuum cleaner. It is easier to see what you are doing with a clean surface, and a vacuum cleaner avoids dust building up in your workshop.

4 As you work down, chisel away the background areas, working inwards from the edges. You can take out slightly bigger chips at this stage, but keep 'planing' along horizontally, going down about ¹⁄₁₆in (2mm) at a time, until you get a smooth even base level with the ½in (13mm) line. Remember that the remaining thickness of stone is only about ⅝in (15mm), so don't whack the chisel down into it or you may crack it and ruin the whole piece.

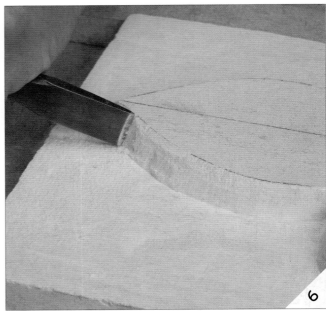

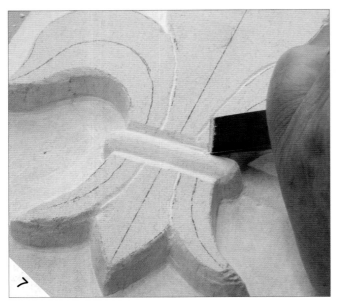

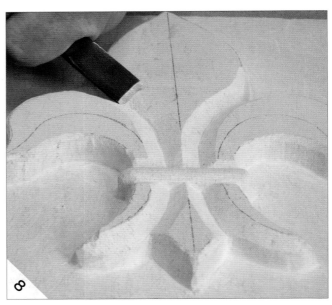

5 You can achieve an even depth to your background by making a simple depth gauge using a screw and a piece of wood. Set the screw so the point protrudes ½in (13mm), place the wood flat on the top surface, and move it all over the lower surface so the screw scratches any areas that are not at the required depth. To obtain a final smooth surface you can, if your stone is soft enough, push the chisel across the surface like a plane.

6 Finish the blocking out by tidying up the vertical edges of the pattern back to the tracing lines. Hold the chisel with its cutting edge almost vertical, and tap it gently along the edge. Always work inwards at the points; an outward cut is likely to break them out.

SHAPING THE FLEUR-DE-LYS

7 Start the detail carving by slightly rounding over the band that holds the three leaves of the lily together. Tap the chisel gently along each edge at a slight angle, remembering to work inwards at the ends.

8 Open out a V between each of the three lily leaves, and work it along the edge of the leaves, still chipping away gently at an angle.

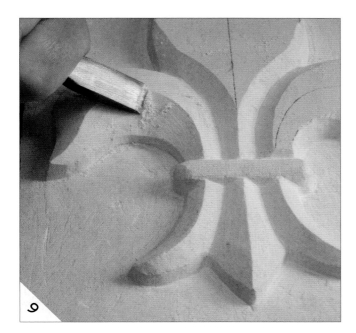

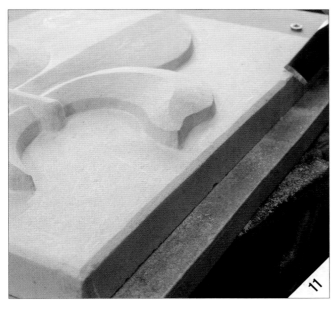

9 Continue this process down the other side of each leaf until you start to form a 'crease' along the centre of the leaf. Take the edges of the leaves down to about ¼in (6mm) from the background. In the inside turns of the leaves, the angle at which the surface presents itself to the chisel increases, so you need to lower the angle of the chisel accordingly.

10 The ridge at the broad middle of each leaf remains at the original thickness of the stone, but as the leaves narrow at the points and through the cross-band, the ridge level is reduced proportionally. Go carefully at the points and remember to work inwards.

FINISHING

11 To finish off, tidy up the edges of the fleur-de-lys, smooth off any unevenness in the background, sharpen up the edge where the pattern meets the background, and finally cut a 45-degree chamfer along the outer edge of the stone.

12 Wash the dust off it and rub it over with a dry cloth to bring up the finish. You can drill a hole in the back with a masonry drill to hang it on a nail, or maybe set it into the brickwork. The stone will survive outdoors indefinitely.

MARBLE IVY PANEL

Marble has been prized for stone carving since ancient times. The decoration on the Parthenon in ancient Athens (see project 9) is well known by its alternative name of the 'Elgin Marbles'. This project is a little more modest, and builds on the experience gained in project 1. It is another incised pattern, but this one has rather more complexity to the incised surface, and it is carved in a marble slab.

Marble is a metamorphic form of limestone (see page 21). It has been compressed and super-heated by the movement of tectonic plates in the Earth's crust, and sometimes by proximity to volcanic magma. This creates a crystalline structure that gives it a degree of translucence not found in ordinary limestone. It is also much harder than limestone but, despite its hardness, it has a weakness – it bruises easily. 'Bruising' in marble occurs when an impact on its surface causes the crystals in the impacted area to partially separate along their adjoining planes. This creates a 'sugary' patch around the point of impact.

A cheap marble paving slab from a garden centre, as I have used for this project, will almost certainly be heavily bruised when you buy it, so any bruises you add will not show as much as they would in a pristine piece of polished marble worktop. Just be careful to tap the chisel along gently and not whack it too hard. Although marble is a hard stone, the method of carving is the same as for softer limestone. You just have to make more passes with the chisel to remove the same amount of material, and be aware that the crystalline nature of marble makes it a little harder to get a crisp edge to the incised pattern.

This pattern is one I designed myself to fit a panel of around 16in (405mm) square. It is an ivy pattern in a style popular in the late Victorian and Edwardian periods. In carving it, you need to follow the gentle flow of the curves and avoid any jarring kinks that may interrupt the movement of the eye. Unlike the house numbers in project 1, the incised surface in this pattern is not a plain V-shape; it is more U-shaped in profile, and the broader leaf sections are given an undulation reflecting natural ivy leaves.

TOOLS
1½lb (655g) dummy mallet • ¼in (6mm) chisel • ½in (13mm) chisel • ¼in (6mm) gouge • ½in (13mm) gouge • ¾in (20mm) gouge • rotary burr tool

MATERIALS
Marble paving slab or worktop off-cut 16in (405mm) square x 1¼in (30mm) thick • wet and dry abrasive (fine-grade) • marble polish

Scale drawing on a 1in (25mm) grid. Enlarge drawing to the required size (see page 10).

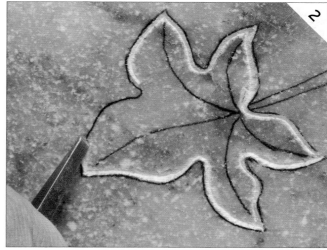

PREPARATIONS

1 Get a marble paving slab, or worktop off-cut if you prefer, ideally 16in (405mm) square x 1¼in (30mm) thick. Make sure the surface is clean and dry. Make a full-size copy of the pattern and trace it onto the marble using carbon paper. A wide thin slab like this could easily crack during carving if not fully supported, so work on a dead-flat surface. A cork pad, such as a cork bathroom mat, will provide a firm cushion to prevent stone chips getting under the slab and creating a potential fracture point.

CARVING THE IVY LEAVES

2 Carefully carve around the inside edge of the guidelines with a small chisel. Tap it along gently with the cutting edge at about 45 degrees to the surface and one of the points penetrating the marble. Take great care not to cause large crystals to flake out at the edges. Keep the chisel sharp.

3 Use a larger chisel to open out deep Vs along the vein lines. Deepen and open out the Vs gradually, keeping the flow of the vein lines as shown on the drawing.

4 Widen the Vs out into a U-shape using ¼in (6mm) and ½in (13mm) gouges. Work carefully up to the edges of the leaves to create a steep edge to the incised area. Re-cut the Vs of the veins even deeper into the bottom of the U, and create an undulating ridge where each 'leaflet' joins the neighbouring part of its leaf. Try to create a natural flow to the leaf surface.

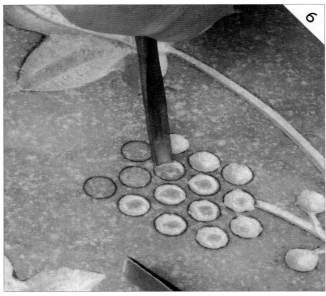

CARVING THE STEMS

5 The flow of the stems is an important feature of the carving. Notice how the stem becomes thicker each time a side stem joins it. Use a small chisel to cut along the edges, taking great care to keep a flowing curve. Cut the narrow stems into a V, but as the stems get wider, use a small gouge to create a U-shaped cross-section. Make the grooves deeper in proportion to the width, and take care to make the grooves of the side stems flow smoothly into the main stem.

CARVING THE BERRIES

6 Ivy has hard berries that cluster loosely on thin stems. Getting them to look right is not easy because they are round. Geometrical shapes are always harder for the carver because any observer can see if a circle is not circular. Use

a ¼in (6mm) gouge to mark around the edge of each circle, cutting inwards towards the centre. Cut carefully and gently so you don't cause a 'sugary' patch outside the circle.

7 To deepen the circle, chip out the middle with a ¼in (6mm) chisel. Place one point of the cutting edge in the centre of the depression, then rotate the cutting edge (and yourself) around the circle right up to the guideline. Repeat the process with the ¼in (6mm) gouge until you have produced a neat hemispherical depression in the marble.

8 To achieve a really neat finish, you need to switch to a rotary multi-tool with an abrasive ball head. Grind the rotating ball carefully into the depression until you have a neat circle.

FINISHING

9 The guidelines can be difficult to remove, and your marble would probably benefit from a polish, so it is worth going over the surface with a very fine 'wet and dry' abrasive. It is important to keep a crisp edge to the carving, so use the abrasive either with a flat vibrating sander or wrap it around a flat piece of wood. Wet the surface thoroughly when using the abrasive, and wash it clean afterwards.

10 Incised carvings rely on shadows and contrasting surfaces to show up the pattern. It is worth using marble polish (available from home improvement stores) to put a shine on the flat surface to contrast with the rougher texture of the incised pattern. Make sure the surface is thoroughly dry, and apply the polish with a cloth wrapped round a flat piece of wood to keep it out of the incised pattern. Buff it up to a shine when dry.

11 Position the panel, outdoors or indoors, in a place where the light will strike it obliquely to enhance the shadows.

PART 2

Developing skills with rocky ruins

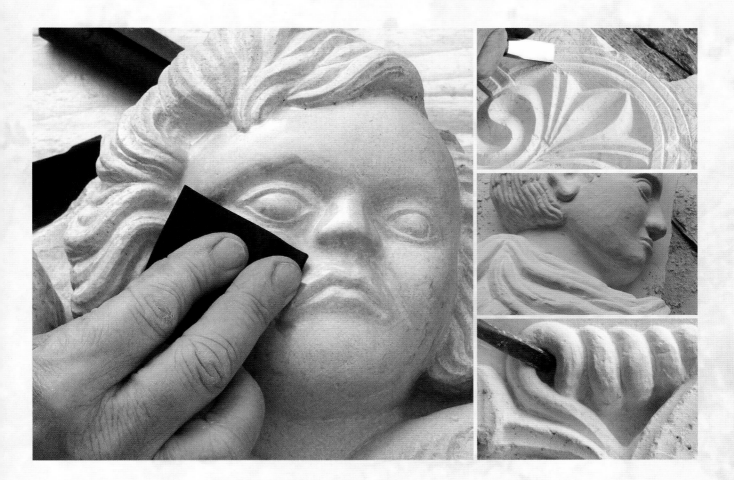

THE IDEA FOR ROCKY RUINS CAME TO me while looking at some holiday photos of the ancient Forum in Rome. I was struck by the charming decorative effect of ruins. A fragment of a once-grand building, lying randomly among a heap of rocks, has a haunting beauty that is almost greater than a complete building. I imagined such fragments scattered in my own garden, as though some ancient lost city had occupied the site before me.

For a hobby stone carver, rocky ruins bring a multitude of benefits. They provide a medium to develop your skills by practising on cheap rockery stone, which you can buy easily from most garden centres. They also allow you to try out the traditional styles of decorative carving used on buildings over the last few thousand years without the trouble and expense (and difficulties with the planning authorities) of constructing a whole cathedral, triumphal arch or Greek temple in your back garden. Best of all, it doesn't matter too much if you break bits off while practising – it is meant to be a ruin.

Most of us live not too far from a garden centre selling lumps of cheap rough stone for rockeries. If you are really lucky, you may live near a limestone quarry. The medium-soft limestones, like the Cotswold stone sold in England, or your nearest local equivalent, are a low-cost option for developing your stone-carving skills.

Rockery stone will vary greatly in quality, even in the same batch. Like many problems, this is also an opportunity, as you will gain a lot of experience in the nature of stone. You will encounter soft spots, hard spots, blast cracks, fault lines and inconveniently placed fossils, and you will be richer for the experience.

Each rock you buy will be uniquely shaped, so you will have to align the drawing to get the best fit. Let the pattern run over its natural edges as if it has been broken centuries after it was carved. It may confuse an archaeologist who digs it up in a thousand years, but the decorative effect in your garden will be quite delightful.

Project 4

NORMAN FRIEZE

The Normans were Vikings with social aspirations. While their fellow Norsemen were wreaking havoc and destruction up and down the coasts of Britain and Western Europe, the Normans followed the path of many later social climbers, and put on French airs.

After repeated Viking raids on the northern part of France in the 9th century, the French king decided to do a deal with them. In 912 AD, Charles the Simple (the clue is in the name) offered them the large tract of land we now call Normandy in return for their nominal allegiance to France. The Normans became de facto rulers of Normandy, and married into the French nobility. The infrastructure that had made the French lords rich now made the Normans rich. It was such a successful arrangement (for the Normans) that they famously extended their franchise, in 1066, to include England.

The remarkable thing about the Normans is the speed with which they became not only 'civilized', but also French. Within a generation they had adopted the language and culture of the people they had conquered. They were no longer 'Norsemen' but 'Normandes'. They spoke with the nasal inflections of the French language, instead of the guttural tones of a Viking. But most of all, they started to build like Frenchmen. They built castles, cathedrals and abbeys, not of wood and mud, but of stone.

The Norman buildings of the early Middle Ages, both in Normandy and England, followed the Romanesque style that had spread across Europe during Charlemagne's Holy Roman Empire in the preceding two centuries. It took its inspiration, as its name suggests, from the Roman buildings that remained from the original Roman Empire of classical times. Romanesque buildings had very thick solid walls, semicircular arches and stout round columns. Surface decoration was usually seen in the form of repeated geometrical patterns such as chevrons and dog's-tooth dentils.

The design for this project, the first of the Rocky Ruins, is from 11th-century England, when the Romanesque style still dominated. It comes from the church (now cathedral) of St Saviour's, Southwark (London), as illustrated in *Pugin's Gothic Ornament*. It is a fairly simple incised pattern to start us off. Most of the carving can be done with a ½in (13mm) chisel. The points at each end of the chisel edge do most of the work and are capable of carving very fine detail if you tap it along gently.

TOOLS
1½lb (655g) dummy mallet • 2½lb (1175g) club hammer • marble point/punch • ¾in (20mm) claw chisel • 2in (50mm) bolster/pitcher • ¼in (6mm) chisel • ½in (13mm) chisel • ¼in (6mm) gouge

MATERIALS
Limestone rockery stone

Scale drawing on a 1in (25mm) grid. Enlarge drawing to the required size (see page 10).

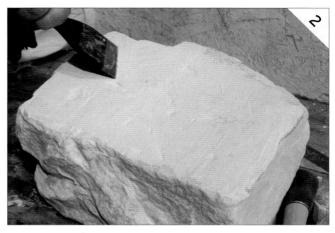

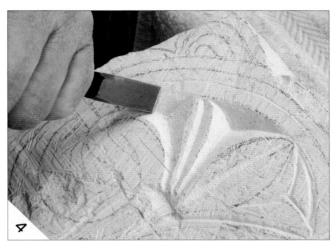

PREPARATIONS

1 This is an incised pattern on a flat surface, so choose a piece of limestone with a flattish face on one side. Test the stone with the point of a chisel when you buy it. You should be able to score a mark in it by hand pressure alone, but if it crumbles into a chalky powder it is too soft. It needs to hold a sharp edge when carved. Rock with a weathered face will be harder than a piece fresh from below ground.

2 The surface needs to be dead flat, so take this opportunity to practise dressing a block of stone (see page 27). Use a point and a claw chisel to rough it out level, then smooth it off with a bolster. The angle of the chisel depends on how hard the stone is – the harder it is, the steeper the angle. Check the flatness in all directions with a steel rule.

3 Make a copy of the pattern so the frieze reaches nearly to the top and bottom edges of the stone and runs over at each end. Tracing onto stone with carbon paper is not easy, but it is still the best way of transferring a complex pattern. Wash off all the dust and wipe the surface hard with a cloth. Dry it thoroughly. Fix the pattern over the stone and carbon paper by taping right around the block with masking tape (the tape will not stick to stone). Press hard with a pencil to trace the pattern onto the stone.

CARVING THE PATTERN

4 You will have a maze of blue lines, so clarify the pattern by marking with a crayon the lines that show the bottom of a V. Start carving with a ½in (13mm) chisel by opening out the Vs between the leaves and the upper semicircle. Start in the middle of each V and tap the chisel along with short sharp taps, holding it at an angle of about 45 degrees with the point digging in. Work outwards, holding this angle, until you are running alongside the ridge lines, by which time the V will have become deeper in proportion to its width.

5 Carry on around, refining the line of the sharp ridges and the bottom of the Vs. When you get to the lower half, mark out all the V lines with the chisel before proceeding so you don't confuse a ridge line with a hollow. The sharp turns in the V of the middle leaves are made by rotating the chisel as you tap it so one point stays in the centre of the turn as the other side turns around the ridge.

6 Complete the carving of the ridges and hollows in the bottom portion, and chamfer in the baseline of the frieze. If your stone is pitted in places, as mine was, this is fine for a Rocky Ruin – just carve through it as if the stone was there when carved and has been knocked out later by the ravages of time. Now turn your attention to the upper semicircles. Cut a small V between each semicircle, taking care with the flow of the curve, then round over the convex profile all the way around each one.

7 Repeat the process on the next segment of the frieze, running the pattern over the edges of the rock as if it has been broken off centuries after being carved. Now carve the central link bands with their little round 'pellets'. All this can be done with the same ½in (13mm) chisel, but a ¼in (6mm) gouge is useful on the pellets.

8 Finally, carve in the little curly leaves in the spandrels using the points of the ½in (13mm) chisel. The chisel can also be used like a plane to go over the carving, tidying up and smoothing the surfaces (this sharpens the chisel at the same time). Make sure the chamfer line at the top and bottom of the frieze is straight.

9 The piece is now finished. Wash off all the dust and place it in your garden, where it will look like a fragment of a ruined Norman church. I keep expecting the Dean of Southwark to come and ask for it back!

AMBITIOUS BISHOPS

In medieval times, the main employment for stone carvers was in decorating religious buildings. The other stone buildings around at the time – castles and a few private houses – did not require much decoration. Religion, however, was big business, and a lot of people made their living from it.

Religion, politics and power were closely related in Norman times. If you couldn't be an earl or a duke, the next best thing was to be a bishop, an abbot, or better still, an archbishop. To show that you were better than the average abbot or bishop, you needed an abbey or cathedral that was better

than the average. The grand abbeys and cathedrals that we see today were mostly commissioned by the ambitious abbots and bishops of the medieval period.

ROMAN
FRIEZE

I have a soft spot for the ancient Romans because I grew up among them. Well, not literally, obviously, but their remains and artefacts were all around me. I live near Colchester, England; the first capital city of Roman Britain. When the Romans launched their invasion of Britain in 43 AD, the place they headed for was Colchester – the Celtic settlement of Camulodunum, as it was then. Camulodunum was so important that when the Roman army reached it, the Emperor Claudius came all the way from Rome to claim the glory of conquering it.

Colchester still has its Roman town walls today. They were built in the first century AD, but not until after Queen Boudicca (or Boadicea as we used to know her) had sacked the town and slaughtered the Roman inhabitants. At the end of the 2,000-year-old high street (where I worked for 32 years) stands a Norman castle, built on the foundations of the Roman temple of Claudius (he made himself a god – good career move!). The temple was destroyed when Boudicca torched it, together with several hundred Roman citizens who had taken refuge inside it.

Stone carving has such a long history that the Roman period is actually nearer to modern times than it is to the beginning of the craft. It can seem nearer still because Classical styles have dominated the design of buildings and their decoration for much of the past 300 years.

The Roman period provides a living inspiration for these Rocky Ruins. At many sites throughout Europe, the Middle East and North Africa you can see fragments of buildings carved with Roman decoration, but none more so than in the epicentre of that great empire – the city of Rome itself.

This pattern comes from the epicentre of the epicentre – the Forum of ancient Rome. You can see it for yourself, encircling the base of what was once a great column. It curves around a circle of about 4 feet (120cm) diameter, curving inwards towards the top. Like project 4, it is another decorated frieze, but this pattern is raised above the background. It gives you practice in carving low relief, where you must carve away the background before shaping the detail.

TOOLS

1½lb (655g) dummy mallet • 2½lb (1175g) club hammer • marble point/punch • ³⁄₄in (20mm) claw chisel • 2in (50mm) bolster/pitcher • ³⁄₁₆in (4mm) chisel • ¼in (6mm) chisel • ½in (13mm) chisel • ¼in (6mm) gouge • ½in (13mm) gouge

MATERIALS

Limestone rockery stone

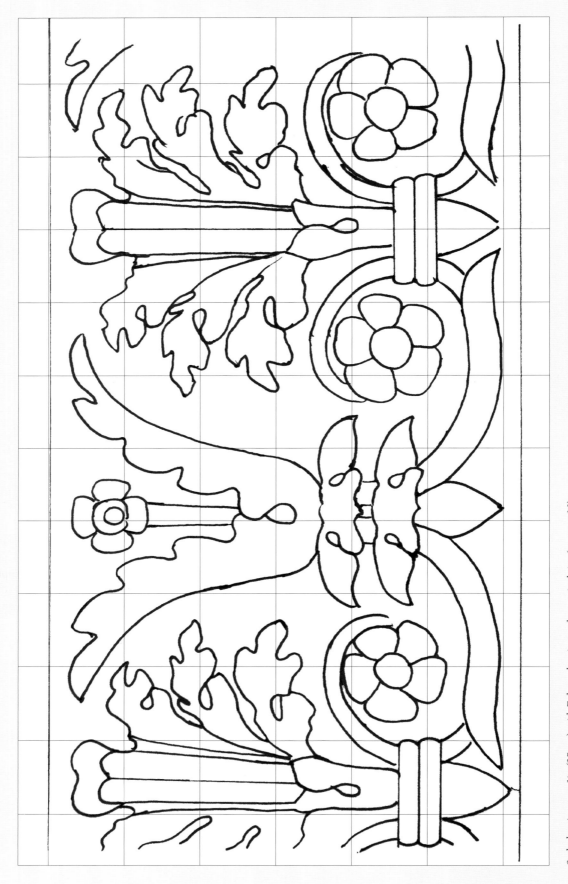

Scale drawing on a 1in (25mm) grid. Enlarge drawing to the required size (see page 10).

PREPARATIONS

1 This carving is made on a curved surface that wraps around the base of a column and slopes inwards at the same time, so choose a piece of stone where one side can easily be shaped to this profile. Make a full-size copy of the pattern so it just about fits the height of the rock. Using a long piece of wood with a pencil inserted through it, or a large compass, draw a segment of a circle with a radius of 2ft (60cm) on a piece of card to create a template with a curve similar to the original column base.

2 Use a point tool and claw chisel to rough out the face of the rock to a consistent curve, checking against the profile card, with another curve at right angles towards the top based on the same profile. As with all the Rocky Ruins, work right over the edges of the rock wherever they happen to fall.

3 Level off the surface with a bolster, and a rasp if necessary, to create a smooth surface onto which you can trace the pattern. Work it as accurately as you can to the profile of the template. Although the whole surface will be carved, you will achieve a better result if you start from the correct profile, just as our Roman mason would have done.

4 Trace or draw the pattern onto the rock, making sure the vertical elements of the pattern are adjusted to take account of the inward vertical curve of the face. You will need to tape right around the rock to hold the tracing in place. Make sure the surface of the rock is dry and free of dust if you are using carbon paper.

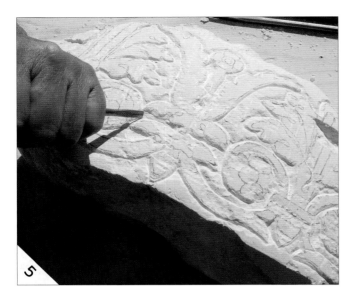

CARVING THE PATTERN

5 Start carving by marking along the edges of the pattern with a small chisel, much like the incised carving in previous projects. This helps to delineate the pattern and protect its edges as you excavate the background.

6 Block out the pattern by chiselling out the background to a depth of ⅜in (10mm), mainly using a ¼in (6mm) chisel. Work down until the sides of the raised parts of the pattern are almost vertical and the bottom is flat. Check the depth with a simple depth gauge made by inserting a screw through a flat piece of wood, protruding to the required depth. On the narrower gaps you will not be able to excavate to the full depth at this stage. Make sure the background follows the curve of the original surface, especially at the top and bottom.

7 Carefully carve the leaves of the flower that fills the centre of the carving. Most of the elements of this carving have an 'escarpment' profile with one sloping edge and one vertical edge, so round over the sloping sides as appropriate. When this is done you can access the background better to level off the surfaces.

8 Carve the acanthus leaves that will flow over the ends of your rock on either side of the main flower, taking care to create a natural flow upwards and outwards from the stem. You can form the little holes (or 'eyes'), which are a typical acanthus feature, by inserting a small sharp screwdriver vertically and twisting it back and forth to drill down about ⅛in (3mm). Notice how I have dealt with the ends of the rock and the blast crack on the right-hand side by carving over them as if the fractures were caused centuries after the carving was made.

9 Carve the curling tendrils and remaining features around the flower heads. Carefully shape the petals of each flower and round over the 'stamen' with a ½in (13mm) gouge. These petals can be quite fragile, so carve carefully.

10 When the pattern is carved, go over the background again to level it off and undercut slightly to create sharp edges where the pattern meets the background. Wash off all the dust and place it in your garden, where you will have your own little piece of ancient Rome.

REAL ROCKY RUINS

Sourcing designs for your own Rocky Ruins is easy if you take a camera on your travels. The ancient Forum in Rome is the perfect place to see Rocky Ruins in their natural environment. What will strike you as marvellous is not just the standard of carving that our ancestors achieved 2,000 years ago, but the scale of construction. Without the aid of tower cranes, they could erect stone columns as high as a four-storey building, placing massively heavy sections on top of one another in perfect alignment using only wooden scaffolding, ropes and pulleys.

Everything would be cut with absolute accuracy from wooden templates to make each three-dimensional stone fit perfectly into its place in an arch, column or dome. The pinnacle of achievement in stone carving and masonry was reached a very long time ago, and two millennia later we can only try to emulate the masons of Ancient Rome.

GRAPEVINE FRIEZE

Mankind's love of wine goes back a long way, which probably explains the perennial popularity of the grapevine as a decorative motif. It occurs throughout the Classical period of the ancient Greeks and Romans, and again from the Renaissance through to the modern day. It is also one of the few Classical forms to be used in Gothic decoration throughout the Middle Ages. There are many medieval examples illustrated in Pugin's Gothic Ornament.

We usually associate wine with the revels and debauchery of the Roman god Bacchus, so it may seem surprising that the grapevine occurs so frequently in Gothic cathedrals and churches in England. But before Henry VIII fell out with the Pope in 1533, all English churches were Roman Catholic, and sacramental wine was used daily. Also, before the climate suddenly became colder in the 14th century, England had plenty of vineyards, so the vine was a familiar feature. Monasteries (and there were many of them before Henry shut them down) were heavily engaged in the production of wine, both for sacramental uses and domestic consumption.

When the Renaissance finally got under way in England in the 17th century, and Roman styles came back into fashion, only a few minor adjustments were needed to change the Gothic grapevine to a more fluid Renaissance version. I have set this design somewhere in the transition from Gothic to Renaissance.

It is adapted from a Tudor house in Eye, Suffolk, England. The original is carved in oak under a pretty oriel window, but I have adapted this to a form more appropriate to a Rocky Ruin – a stone string-course.

A string-course is a horizontal layer of stones running the length of a wall, usually separating the various 'storeys' of the building. It is frequently decorated, and occurs in all styles of architecture. It usually projects outwards with a sloping top surface to throw water off the side of the building, and curves back under with an *ovolo* (convex) or *cavetto* (concave) moulding.

This project takes relief carving to the next level. It is deeply hollowed and undercut, with a pattern that is almost three-dimensional. There is an element of 'destruction testing' here. You will learn how far you can undercut before the edge starts to break up, and you may lose a few pieces, so a Rocky Ruin is just the thing to practise on.

TOOLS

1½lb (655g) dummy mallet • 2½lb (1175g) club hammer • marble point/punch • ¾in (20mm) claw chisel • 2in (50mm) bolster/pitcher • ³⁄₁₆in (4mm) chisel • ¼in (6mm) chisel • ½in (13mm) chisel • ¾in (20mm) chisel • ¼in (6mm) gouge • ½in (13mm) gouge • ¾in (20mm) gouge • ³⁄₈in (10mm) masonry drill bit

MATERIALS

Limestone rockery stone

Scale drawing on a 1in (25mm) grid. Enlarge drawing to the required size (see page 10).

PREPARING THE STRING-COURSE MOULDING

1 Make a full-size copy of the drawing. Trace the end profile of the ovolo moulding onto a sheet of card and cut out the profile to produce a template. This will be used to dress the rock for carving.

2 Use a rock that is at least 6in (150mm) thick and that will accommodate the string-course moulding. Draw straight lines on the rock top and bottom to line up the edges of the string-course. Remove rock with a point, claw and bolster until you have produced a smooth moulding that fits the side profile template. Lay pieces of 3in (75mm) timber on the top and bottom of the moulding to check they are parallel from the front and underneath.

3 Tracing the pattern onto the rock with carbon paper is easier if you create a smooth surface with abrasives, wash the dust off, and dry it thoroughly. Fix the tracing paper in place by taping right around the rock and back again – the tape will not stick to stone. Trace on the pattern and go over it with a hard pencil if necessary. The background of the string-course moulding is a concave cavetto moulding, which is the reverse of the ovolo on the front. Cut out a template along the dotted line shown on the drawing, and mark this line on the ends of the rock.

ROUGHING OUT THE CARVING

4 Because the pattern has a number of near-circular 'eyes' in the leaves, which are cut to a depth of up to 1½in (40mm), it is best to start by drilling these almost to depth with a ⅜in (10mm) masonry drill. Don't go too deep or you will end up with holes in the background. You can also drill out some of the deep narrow gaps to make the chiselling easier. Stone needs somewhere to go when you chisel it, so it can break out into the drill hole.

5 Chisel out the gaps between the pattern elements, mainly with a ³⁄₁₆in (4mm) chisel, and work down towards the cavetto background as far as you reasonably can at this stage. Keep the sides of the pattern elements as near to vertical as possible, otherwise the pattern will spread. Chisel out the background at the top and bottom where it joins the edge fillets.

6 Look at which elements of the pattern are high, medium and low in their respective levels, and mark them H, M and L with a pencil. Work down the vines to the required level with chisels, then rough out the hollows in the leaves with a ¾in (20mm) gouge. Leave the grapes and the curly tendril alone for now.

CARVING THE DETAIL

7 The best place to start the detail carving is with the grapes. Shape them with a small chisel so they are layered naturally at different levels from the foreground to the background. You can use the concave side of a ¾in (20mm) gouge to round them over smoothly. Use a ¼in (6mm) chisel to sharpen the hexagonal joins between each grape, especially the little 'triangles' where the hexagons meet.

8 A natural grapevine has twisting shredded bark that spirals along its length. Create this effect with a ¼in (6mm) gouge, twisting it around the vine as you move along it. The edges along each twisting cove can be left a little rough to simulate the shredded bark. See how the stem of the big leaf flows into the vine.

9 Carve the little curling tendril in the top left. To make it appear as three-dimensional as the shallow space allows, curve it to the left at the top and to the right at the bottom. You can use the concave side of a ½in (13mm) gouge to finish it smoothly.

10 Shape the leaves, mainly using gouges, to create hollows around the edges of the leaves, and deep hollows between the 'eyes' where the leaflets meet. The big leaf is one of the key features of the carving, so focus on getting a natural rise and fall. Put in the leaf veins with the small chisel. Sharpen up the edges of the leaves.

FINISHING

11 Take the background down to its final level, using the dotted line on the template as a guide to create a smooth cavetto moulding behind the carving. On the lower border below the carving, take the level down another ⅛in (3mm) to create a fillet separating the cavetto from the border. Now go around the edges of the pattern, undercutting them so they appear to be separate from the background. Undercut deeply under the grape leaves around the 'eyes' where the leaflets meet. Make sure the stone has a space to break into when you chisel, otherwise you will break bits off the pattern.

12 Tidy up the carving, sharpening up any detail that needs it. Now wash all the dust out of the hollows with a hose, and place the fragment of grapevine string-course in your garden.

Project 7

GOTHIC CROCKET

Around the middle of the 12th century, the cathedral builders of England and France got a bit bored with the old Romanesque style. Its semicircular arches, thick solid walls and stout round columns were starting to look a bit old-fashioned. They wanted something lighter, taller, and with an interior more like a forest glade than a tomb.

The cathedral of Saint-Denis in Paris was one of the first in this new style, but gradually it spread outwards across the realms of France, England and beyond. The style we now know as Gothic had arrived. It survived about 350 years in its medieval incarnation, with another 100 to come in the spectacular Victorian Gothic Revival.

The Gothic church had slim clusters of columns that soared skywards, branching out into stone ribs that met in the middle of the roof, like the branches of the great oaks in the surrounding forests. The capitals of the columns became clusters of curling leaves, but this was still not enough to reflect the glory of nature. The steeply pointed pediments and pinnacles soaring upwards, both inside and outside the building, sprouted leaves in a form unique to the Gothic style – the crocket.

The crocketed finial is one of the most important signature features of Gothic buildings. The crockets – curling leafy projections – are distributed evenly up the steeply rising gables of the finial or pediment. They give the structure an altogether more organic look, bursting with life and energy like the first flush of spring.

This example is adapted from a Victorian Gothic monument at Eye, Suffolk, England, but it is very similar to a medieval example illustrated in *Pugin's Gothic Ornament*. In the drawing I have included part of the gable moulding, but how much of this ends up in the carving (in my case, very little) depends on the size and shape of your rock.

On a cathedral building site, the stones for the gable would have been prepared by a mason, working to accurate templates. The mason would usually leave the crocket blocked out to be finished by the stone carver. I have followed the tradition of templates and 'blocking out for carving' in this project even though we are not producing a complete stone – it still gives the best starting point for carving.

TOOLS
1½lb (655g) dummy mallet ● 2½lb (1175g) club hammer ● marble point/punch ● ³⁄₄in (20mm) claw chisel ● 2in (50mm) bolster/pitcher ● ³⁄₁₆in (4mm) chisel ● ¼in (6mm) chisel ● ½in (13mm) chisel ● ³⁄₄in (20mm) chisel ● ¼in (6mm) gouge ● ½in (13mm) gouge ● ³⁄₄in (20mm) gouge ● stone rasp (optional)

MATERIALS
Limestone rockery stone

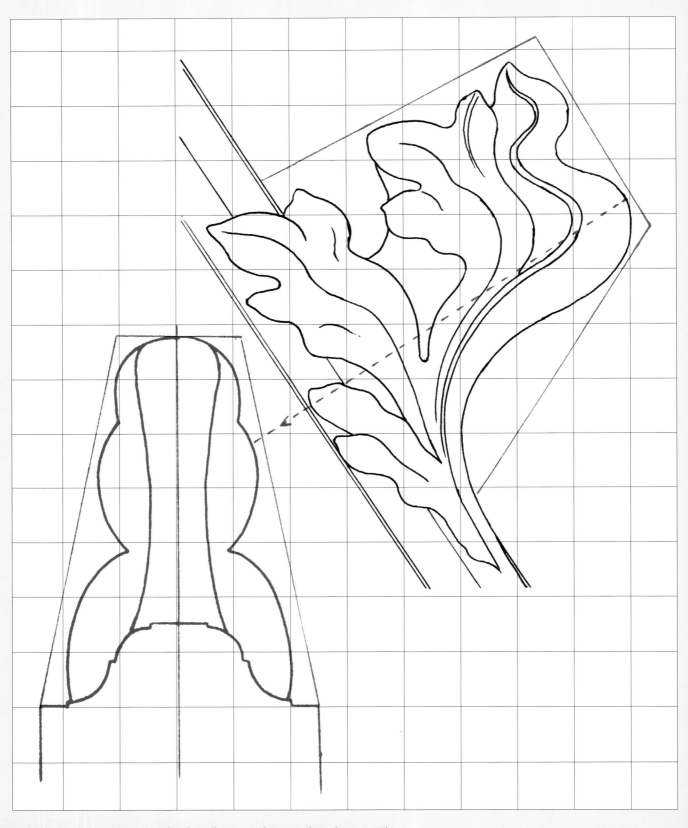

Scale drawing on a 1in (25mm) grid. Enlarge drawing to the required size (see page 10).

DRESSING THE ROCK FOR CARVING

1 Make a full-size copy of the drawing and trace the side pattern and end profile onto a sheet of card. Cut the card to produce templates for the side and end dimensions. You do not need to cut round the detail – just cut out straight lines along the edges of the pattern. These will be used to dress the rock for carving.

2 This project suits a medium-sized wedge-shaped rock. Line up the templates on the rock to find the orientation that will give you as much carved pattern as possible with the minimum of rock to remove. Mark around the edge of the side profile, and start removing rock with a point, claw and bolster until you have squared off the side profile.

3 Repeat the process with the end profile templates. Make sure they are lined up at both ends, and allow for the slope at one end foreshortening the template. Now work down the faces until you have produced a block with smooth surfaces on which to draw the detail carving pattern. As with all the rocky ruins, work straight over the broken edge of the rock.

ROUGHING OUT THE CARVING

4 Re-cut the side template to give an outline of the leaf detail. Draw this onto both sides of the crocket, making sure they are lined up. We are about to enter the roughing-out phase, which in any carving can seem like a lot of hard work. In a three-dimensional carving it can be the majority of the work, but it is an essential part of the job.

5 Re-work the profile of the block to follow the outline of the leaf pattern. This can take some time, and you will find that a stone rasp is helpful for shaping the tips of the leaves. Cut channels to separate each of the main leaf groups. You will need to work these down further as the roughing out progresses.

6 Cut out the part of the end profile that outlines the gable moulding. Whether or not your rock has any room to carve the moulding (mine doesn't), you need to mark where it sits in the pattern, as the lower leaves lay over it. Line it up to a centreline drawn around the block, at the level shown on the drawing, and draw around it.

7 Now we are into the final stage of the roughing out – shaping the 'neck' and sides of the crocket so everything appears to flow upwards and outwards from the gable moulding.

The lower group of leaves lays over the moulding. The middle group retains its full width at the outer end, but narrows inwards and down towards the neck. The upper leaf is narrower than the others and is rounded over at the top and down the neck.

CARVING THE DETAIL

8 Now we come to the most satisfying part of the project – the detail carving. The first step is to excavate the channels between the leaf groups a little deeper, and run the channel lines down into the neck. Then, starting with the middle group of leaves, create a deep hollow across the middle of the leaf. Shape the leaves into this distinctive Gothic 'lumpy' form, flowing into the hollow and out again to give each leaf a pronounced bulge at the end. Carve a large convex 'leaf vein' curling up and down along the leaf and flowing down to the neck; a ¼in (6mm) gouge can be used upside down to finish it off.

9 Repeat the process with the lower group of leaves. They should spring out of the gable moulding at the neck end (if your rock goes back that far); lay about ½in (13mm) above the moulding at the middle, with part of the leaf rising up above the moulding at the far end. At the lower edges of the leaves, cut the gaps into the line of the gable moulding.

10 The uppermost leaf flows up the neck and over the top in a pronounced 'wave'. Extend the flat fillet of the gable moulding all the way up the neck and over the top, with a cove along each side. When you get over the crest of the wave, create a convex vein from the centre line extending out towards either side into two separate leaf points.

11 For the crocket to have a visible form on a high building when seen from ground level, it is necessary for the features to be boldly delineated. Sharpen up all the vein lines and edges, and cut deeply into the channels between the leaf groups. Separate the leaf points on both sides by hollowing out the bulk of stone between them, taking care not to break off the points. Outline the fillet of the gable moulding in the centre of the hollow.

FINISHING

12 Generally tidy up the carving. Pay particular attention to the edges of the gable moulding where they show. Now wash off all the dust and place your 'cathedral fragment' on the rockery.

GOTHIC BOSS

The revolution in the design of churches and cathedrals that started in the 12th century gave us much more than just the crockets in project 7. The thick solid walls of the Romanesque style were replaced with huge windows of coloured glass, flooding light into the interior.

These windows were made possible by a new method of construction that did not require thick walls to support the roof. In a flash of brilliance, medieval masons invented the stone equivalent of the structural steel framework. The weight of the vaulted roof would be borne on slender stone columns, braced on the outside by flying buttresses, spaced equally along the sides of the nave. They would rise from the floor to the impossibly high ceiling before dividing themselves into pointed arches with slender ribs, branching out across the ceiling vault to meet their neighbours from the next column and the opposite side. The outer walls could now be filled with thin stone tracery and decorative glass.

The slender columns were partly an illusion. They were made to look more slender by being subdivided into about four smaller columns, each of these subdivided usually into three more, so that what was a fairly substantial structure appeared to be a group of about a dozen thin columns all tied together. The stones for these were carved as blocks one on top of the other in the traditional manner, with the sub-columns carved into the vertical sides and all matching up by careful use of templates, giving a continuous vertical line to lead the eye heavenwards.

It was what happened at the tops of these columns that gives us the subject of this project. The slender ribs of the lierne vault spread across the underside of the ceiling to join in a structure of thin 'arches' supporting the stone 'web' between them. The point where they met would be decorated with a 'boss' or pendant – the equivalent of a keystone in the arch.

This Gothic boss is from the 12th-century church of St George de Boucherville, Normandy, France, as illustrated in *Pugin's Gothic Ornament*. Its carved foliage decorates the point where six 'ribs' meet. If your rock is big enough, you can include the stumps of the ribs as they protrude from the boss. This is a more three-dimensional carving that will take you deeper into the world of the medieval stonemason.

TOOLS

1½lb (655g) dummy mallet • 2½lb (1175g) club hammer • marble point/punch • ¾in (20mm) claw chisel • 2in (50mm) bolster/pitcher • ³⁄₁₆in (4mm) chisel • ¼in (6mm) chisel • ½in (13mm) chisel • ¾in (20mm) chisel • ¼in (6mm) gouge • ½in (13mm) gouge • ¾in (20mm) gouge • stone rasp (optional) • stone/concrete saw (optional)

MATERIALS

Limestone rockery stone

Scale drawing on a 1in (25mm) grid. Enlarge drawing to the required size (see page 10).

SHAPING THE BOSS

1 This carving suits a rock that is generally dome-shaped and at least 9in (230mm) across by 7in (180mm) thick. If it is too small, you will not have enough stone to make an effective boss.

2 Make up two circular cardboard templates, one of them 4in (100mm) in diameter and the other 9in (230mm) in diameter. Use the 9in (230mm) circle to find the centre of the main mass of rock that will accommodate the whole boss (or as much of it as possible). Use a claw chisel and bolster to level off an area that will accommodate the 4in (100mm) template for the central boss using the same centre point. Draw an accurate 4in (100mm)-diameter circle round this template.

3 Using a ½in (13mm) chisel, cut around the edge of the circle in a gradually widening V. Work the chisel up to the circle line and bring the inner edge up to vertical as the V widens. This is to try to preserve an accurate 4in (100mm) circle as you work down to the next level.

4 Switch to a point (or punch) and a claw chisel as you work outwards from the circle to level off a flat area 1⅛in (28mm) below the top of the small central boss.

5 Take the 9in (230mm) template and cut out the 4in (100mm) centre accurately so that it fits like a doughnut over the centre boss. Draw another circle around this template to outline the 9in (230mm) diameter main boss.

6 Repeat the process of working around this circle and down a further 2¼in (55mm) – now 3⅜in (85mm) below the top of the small central boss. You can use a point/punch and claw chisel or, as I am doing here, you can cut out the bulk with a concrete saw first. It is not really quicker or easier, but it involves less hammering. My rock had a fault line that could have cracked under heavy hammering, and the saw exerts less shock. Stone, for all its hardness, is basically a fragile material.

7 Level off any rock outside the boss and mark in where the vault ribs join the boss (see drawing). There is a ridge rib running along the centre of the vault, and four diagonal ribs that come off it at an angle of around 30 degrees. Each rib line passes through the centre point of the boss (take great care with this) and they meet in two groups of three on opposite sides.

8 Chisel out the sides of the boss where there are no ribs, to continue the cylinder of rock down to the base. Start to separate the individual ribs (where they exist) with a medium to large gouge.

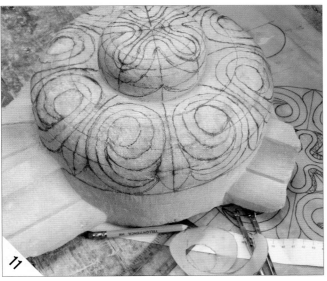

9 Carve the ribs to create a cavetto moulding either side of the 1in (25mm) fillet, then a ⅛in (3mm) vertical fillet, with an ovolo moulding down to the outer edge – an overall width of 5in (125mm) for a complete rib. Where the three ribs merge, mitre the cavettos into one another. Make sure the lines on each rib are straight and parallel; accuracy is vital if you want it to look as if a medieval stonemason had made it.

10 Shape the inner and outer circles into two domes, as illustrated in the drawing. This will form the base for the carving, so after roughing out with the claw, shape it carefully to a smooth regular surface.

CARVING THE MAIN BOSS

11 Draw the pattern onto the stone, taking great care with the geometry. Medieval masons were very accurate and, although this is a Rocky Ruin, it needs to look as if it were carved accurately before it became a ruin. Divide the large and small bosses into eight equal segments, using the ridge rib as your datum and a fabric tape measure to space the segments equally.

12 Start carving the incised pattern by cutting a V along the centre line of each of the straight leaves, then do the same with each of the curved leaves. Gradually open out the V and create a convex curve towards the outer edge of the leaf. Make sure you keep track of which pattern lines are high points and which are low points.

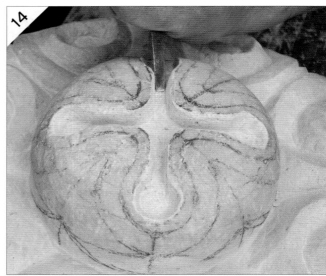

13 Cut a steeper edge on the outside of each leaf, working it to an almost vertical edge about ¼in (6mm) deep. At the lower edge of the pattern, carve a straight chamfer around the base of the circle, level with the top of the ribs.

CARVING THE SMALL BOSS

14 Now carve the detail onto the small centre boss. This is separated into four sections around the form of a cross. Cut out the cross in the centre with a ³⁄₁₆in (4mm) chisel, taking it to a depth of about ⁵⁄₁₆in (8mm).

15 Leave a band of stone ¼in (6mm) wide around the cross you have just cut. Now cut a moulding ¼in (6mm) wide all the way around this shaped like an inverted V. Cut across the V at right angles to form a line of small pyramids. Take care with these, as they can easily crumble and spoil the effect.

16 Finally, form a leaf in the middle of each of the four segments. These are similar to those separating the segments on the main boss, but smaller. Linking these leaves is a sort of 'swag' in an inverted V profile, curving down and under the small boss alongside the row of 'pyramids'. Undercut the swag to separate the small boss from the main boss.

FINISHING

17 Now wash off all the dust and place the finished piece in your garden. What started off as an amorphous lump of rock now looks like something that fell from the roof of a medieval cathedral. It's lucky you weren't underneath it at the time!

THE GLORY OF GOTHIC

The Gothic ribbed vault ceiling is a three-dimensional masterpiece of engineering that would challenge a modern computer-aided design system, yet medieval masons worked it out by drawing flat templates on a plaster floor. After a few mistakes, and several serious collapses, they quite quickly solved the structural problems. By adding flying buttresses (A) on the outside of the building, they could prevent the sides from being forced outwards and the roof collapsing into the nave. This enabled them to create a shallow stone vault that would stay up, supported, apparently, only by slender columns and ribs.

Earlier versions had quite simple pointed arches joined at a boss, like the Gothic choir at Vezelay, France, which is tacked on to the earlier Romanesque nave (B).

Later versions became more elaborate, like the magnificent 14th-century fan vault found at Sherborne, England (C), with its 75 decorated bosses. The best, and last, of the great fan vaults was built around 1530 for Kings College Chapel, Cambridge, England.

The Victorian Gothic Revival made full use of the ribbed vault and Gothic boss, but the great days of cathedral building were long gone. This Victorian

example from the chapel at Tyntesfield, England, illustrates a configuration of ribs and bosses very similar to the one in this project (D).

So next time you go into a Gothic cathedral, don't forget to look up and marvel that the hundreds of tons of stone in the roof above your head stay exactly where the medieval mason put them.

Project 9

PARTHENON FRAGMENT

The Parthenon sculptures from ancient Athens, better known in Britain as the 'Elgin Marbles',
have in their 2,500-year history seen foreign armies and foreign rulers come and go, from the
ancient Romans to the more recent Turks. They have suffered one indignity after another,
but none so devastating as those heaped on them in the 17th and 18th centuries.

It seems nobody cared much about the Parthenon or its sculptures after the decline of ancient Greece, and the figures were defaced by early Christian iconoclasts. When a besieged Turkish garrison in 1687 were looking for a place to store their gunpowder and make a stand against their attackers, they chose the Parthenon. Predictably, a cannonball struck the gunpowder magazine, causing an explosion that was devastating both to the building and the garrison. The ancient temple became an ancient ruin in a few seconds.

It was all downhill from there. The locals used the ruins as a stone quarry, and many carved stones were burned to make lime. The destruction continued for more than a hundred years until, in 1801, enter Lord Elgin, the British ambassador.

Elgin was horrified by the destruction of such historic artworks and was determined to save them. By loosely interpreting a permit from the Turkish governor to remove artefacts from the Parthenon, he removed most of the remaining sculptures and friezes between 1801 and 1812 (not without further damage) and shipped them to England.

The artworks have spent the past 200 years in the British Museum, their decline halted at last. The Greeks want them back, and look upon Lord Elgin's 'rescue' as an act of theft. The British Museum says, perhaps with some justification, that if the sculptures had not been 'taken into care' by Lord Elgin they probably would not exist today.

This extract from the south frieze procession shows the head and shoulders of a young cowherd driving the sacred cattle. We will be carving (in limestone – not marble) to a depth of about 2½in (60mm), so this is an exercise in high relief, but also in figurative sculpture. It leads us into carving facial features, the texture of hair and the folds of drapery – practice that will come in useful later when tackling small statues.

TOOLS
1½lb (655g) dummy mallet • 2½lb (1175g) club hammer • marble point/punch • ¾in (20mm) claw chisel • 2in (50mm) bolster/pitcher • ³⁄₁₆in (4mm) chisel • ¼in (6mm) chisel • ½in (13mm) chisel • ¾in (20mm) chisel • ¼in (6mm) gouge • ½in (13mm) gouge • ¾in (20mm) gouge • stone rasp (optional)

MATERIALS
Limestone rockery stone • wet and dry abrasive (fine-grade)

Scale drawing on a 1in (25mm) grid. Enlarge drawing to the required size (see page 10).

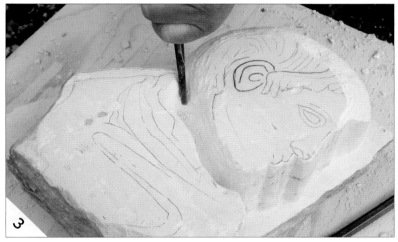

PREPARATIONS

1 Get a fairly broad piece of rock and level off the opposite faces to produce a slab at least 5in (125mm) thick – thicker if possible. Dress the top face to a smooth surface (see page 27) so you can trace the pattern onto it. Make a full-size copy of the pattern. Align it so it gives the best fit to the block of stone, put some carbon paper under it, and tape the tracing securely in place. The tape will not stick to the stone, so wrap it right around the block and stick it to both edges of the tracing. Trace the pattern onto the stone.

ROUGHING OUT

2 Draw a line around the sides of the block 2½in (60mm) from the front face. Chip away all the stone outside the pattern lines down to this depth. Straighten up the edges so they are vertical from the outside edge of the pattern, otherwise the pattern will spread outwards as you work down. Level off the background area at 2½in (60mm).

3 Round over the top and back of the head into a foreshortened three-dimensional form. Work this round to the neck, and lower the level of the middle of the neck to about 1in (25mm) below the original surface. Leave the face, jawline and ear untouched for now.

4 The perspective of the shoulders is foreshortened to appear deeper than it really is. The cowherd's right shoulder is the most forward point, and the front and back are rounded away from it. Try to imagine the anatomy of the shoulder as far as the design allows, and leave enough stone to carve the drapery folds later. Layer the upper levels of the robe towards the neck to help the foreshortened perspective.

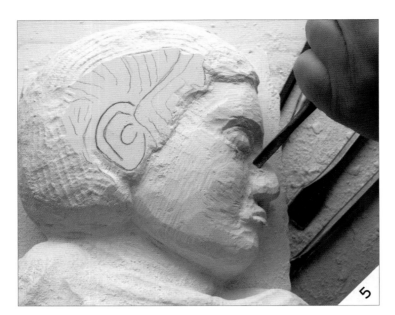

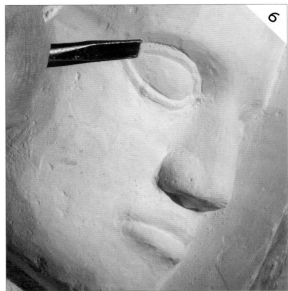

CARVING THE DETAIL

5 Form the shape of the face to get the key facial features the right size and in the right place. The face is in profile and the ear is the highest point on the carving. Shape the jawline from the ear down to the chin and neck. Create a hollow around the eye and down the side of the nose – the tip of the nose is about 1½in (40mm) below the original surface. Shape the forehead and eyebrows, taking care that the nose joins them in the right place. Shape the chin, and hollow out beneath it down into the folds of the drapery. Keep standing the piece upright as you work to check the effect.

6 Now carve the detail into the eyes, nose and lips. This is the tricky part. A slight difference in these features can completely change the expression on the face. Proceed carefully, and don't remove too much stone until you are sure everything is in the right place. Use a hard pencil to draw in a detail before cutting so you can see how it will look. Notice how the adolescent cowherd has a rather sulky expression. Use a ¼in (6mm) gouge to hollow around the eyes and nostrils, and the corner point of a ¼in (6mm) chisel to cut in the sharp lines of the eyelids, eyebrows and the join of the lips.

7 Shape the ear with the ¼in (6mm) gouge. Define the edge of the hairline, and finish shaping the forehead, eyebrows, cheekbone, jawline and chin. A stone rasp is useful for moulding the more rounded features.

8 Now the face is done we can undercut the edges all around the head and body. The aim is to make the figure appear detached from the background when viewed from the front. You can take the background a bit deeper if it needs it, and work it to a smooth level finish.

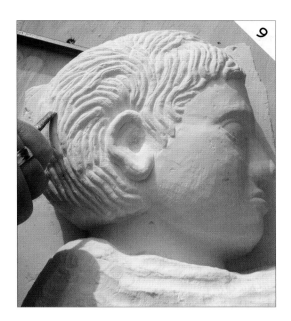

9 To create the hair texture, remember that hair is arranged in levels – first there are waves, then curls within the waves, then hairs within the curls. There is a limit to how far you can go with this in a fairly small stone carving, but I have tried to follow the original. You can do most of the work with the concave side of a ¼in (6mm) gouge.

10 The robe is of loose cloth that wraps from the back around the neck, continuing round the shoulder to where it hangs down the back again. It might help to try arranging a thick piece of cloth in this manner to get a better visual idea of how it flows and falls. Hollow out the fold in front of the throat with a ³⁄₁₆in (4mm) chisel. Carve the folds smaller and closer together in the parts nearest the neck to enhance the perspective. Use both sides of your gouges to shape the folds. A stone rasp will come in useful to shape the broader areas.

11 The Parthenon sculptures have a fairly glossy finish, being carved in marble. We can create this by polishing with fine abrasives (see page 31). Wet the surface and go over it with 180-grit wet and dry abrasive. Follow this with finer grades, up to at least 600-grit, washing the slurry off often. This should produce a smooth finish with a fine satin sheen.

12 Wash off all the dust and slurry. You should now have a carving with an appearance similar to marble that will look good in your garden, or even inside your house.

95

BAROQUE ANGEL FACE

The Baroque style, which dominated the 17th century, was arguably the peak of human achievement in architecture and the decorative arts. Like most of the great styles, it started in religious buildings before being taken up by the secular world. Also like most great styles, it started in Italy before spreading across the rest of Europe.

One of the key figures in the development of the Italian Baroque was Francesco Borromini (1599–1667). He came from a family of stonemasons in northern Italy and was himself a highly skilled stone carver, but he is chiefly remembered as the architect and 'interior designer' of several of the great Baroque churches built in Rome in the 17th century.

Borromini was greatly inspired by the work of Michelangelo in the previous century, so it is no surprise that sculptural forms figure highly in his buildings. In particular, he loved winged cherub heads, which became almost his signature piece. They occur everywhere throughout his buildings, on capitals and cornices, in spandrels and niches, and looking down from his magnificent domes onto the visitors below. Some of the finest examples are in the dome of Sant'Ivo della Sapienza in Rome, and they provide the inspiration for this Rocky Ruin.

Borromini's angels are serene, child-like and cute. They have inspired millions of plaster cherub ornaments in modern homes. This example, with his round chubby face, broad forehead and wild hair, is typical of Borromini's style. He looks down from a spandrel in a dome – just a head and shoulders with angel wings spreading either side of him. Unless you have a very large rock, you will have no room for more than just the stumps of the wings, so I have not included complete wings or any architectural mouldings on the drawing: the head is the main subject.

There is a strange codicil to the tale of Borromini in the 20th-century Cold War. One of the best biographies of Borromini was written by Sir Anthony Blunt, a respected art historian and art advisor to Queen Elizabeth II. The biography was published in 1979 – just as Blunt was exposed as a Soviet spy!

TOOLS
1½lb (655g) dummy mallet • 2½lb (1175g) club hammer • marble point/punch • ¾in (20mm) claw chisel • 2in (50mm) bolster/pitcher • ³⁄₁₆in (4mm) chisel • ¼in (6mm) chisel • ½in (13mm) chisel • ¾in (20mm) chisel • ¼in (6mm) gouge • ½in (13mm) gouge • ¾in (20mm) gouge • stone rasp (optional)

MATERIALS
Limestone rockery stone
• wet and dry abrasive (fine-grade)

Scale drawing on a 1in (25mm) grid. Enlarge drawing to the required size (see page 10).

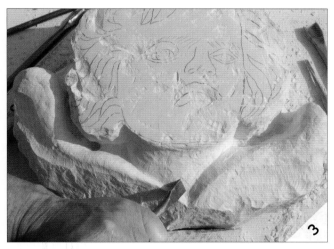

PREPARATIONS

1 Get a piece of rock at least 6in (150mm) thick and dress the top face to a smooth surface. Make a full-size copy of the pattern and align it so it gives the best fit to the block of stone. Trace the pattern onto the stone with carbon paper and tidy it up with a hard pencil. This is a three-dimensional carving, so the flat pattern is just a guide to help us place the main features in the right position.

ROUGHING OUT

2 Draw a line around the sides of the head area about 4in (100mm) from the front face. Carefully remove all the stone outside the pattern lines down to this depth and level off the background area. The narrow gap between the hair, neck and wings is difficult to excavate. Drill out a line of holes with a masonry drill before chiselling it out, and continue to work it to depth as you reduce the surrounding areas later.

3 Rough out the shape of the neck. Leave enough stone under the chin for a bit of a 'double chin' later. In roughing out the wings and shoulders you have some flexibility depending on the shape of your rock. My rock slopes away sharply at the bottom, so I have tilted the wings downwards, which suits a downward-looking angel (Borromini always adapted the wings to suit the situation).

4 The head is now easier to see, so we can start to rough it into shape by rounding over the outside of the face and reducing the level of the hair. Notice how the head tilts slightly to the right and down, so try to reflect this in the roughing out. As you rough the hair into shape, take the opportunity to practise forming it into natural flowing curls.

CARVING THE DETAIL

5 With the face now easier to visualize, we can shape the main facial features. The tip of the nose remains at the original surface, so use gouges and chisels to create a hollow between the nose and upper lip, and hollows up the side of the nose into the corners of the eyes. Carve the shape of both eyes, with the angel's left eye (on your right) lower than the other to suit the tilt of the head. Shape the lips to face the same way. Reshape the head and hair as you go to achieve the full three-dimensional effect.

6 Now carve the fine detail into the eyes, nose and lips. Don't forget that a slight difference in these features can completely change the expression on the face, so proceed carefully. Use a hard pencil to draw in a detail before cutting so you can see how it will look. Use the corner point of a ¼in (6mm) chisel to cut in the sharp lines of the eyelids, eyebrows and the join of the lips.

7 Shape the forehead, eyebrows, cheeks and chin to fit in with the eyes, nose and mouth. Try to achieve the baby-face effect by keeping everything soft and rounded, with a bit of a double chin. Keep standing the piece upright as you work to check the effect. Finish the face back to the hairline, and reshape the neck.

8 The curls in the angel's hair are much more pronounced than those in project 9. They fall into very distinct groups of waves, curls and wisps. They flow from the edges of the face and tumble down towards the neck and the background. The drawing shows you how they should look from the front, but you have to work out for yourself the three-dimensional flow into the background. Use the pencil to see how a curl will look before you start cutting with the ¼in (6mm) chisel and gouge.

100

9 Refine the shape of the wings, and carve the feathers with the ¼in (6mm) chisel and a ½in (13mm) gouge. Draw in the feathers first to get a natural bird-like formation before cutting them. The wings are not just stuck on the back of the shoulders; the feathers encase the angel's body like a cloak from the neck down. The size and shape of your rock will determine how much of the wings you will be able to include.

FINISHING

10 With the detail carving finished, we can undercut the edges all around the head and wings. The aim is to make the figure appear detached from the background, so take the background a bit deeper if it needs it and work it to a smooth level finish. The narrow gap between the wings and hair is difficult to get at with chisels, so it helps if you drill in from the side first to undermine the channel.

11 The angel needs very smooth skin, so polish the limestone with several grades of fine wet and dry abrasive as in project 9, finishing with at least 600-grit. Keep washing the paste off frequently as you work. This should produce a smooth finish with a fine satin sheen.

12 Wash off all the dust and slurry. Your angel should now look truly angelic, and is ready to look serenely down on you, or up at you, depending on where you put it.

101

PART 3

Decorative carvings in the round

AFTER THE FIRST TEN PROJECTS YOU will have done your 'basic training' in stone carving and will have created ten carvings that I hope you will be proud to put on display in your home and garden. You will now be ready to move on to the next stage: making free-standing decorative objects from 'proper' carving stone.

Up till now you will not have had to spend much money on this hobby of stone carving – just a fairly small outlay on a few tools and some cheap rocks – but to move up to the next stage you may need to invest in some lifting equipment (see page 24) and pay a bit more for your stone. Find a source for blocks of good-quality carving limestone (see pages 22–23) and sort out the logistics of transporting it (or getting it delivered) to your home and handling it when you get it there. Be nice to your stone supplier and he or she may let you have the sizes you want at 'off-cut' prices. The practice you will have had in the first ten projects will ensure your expenditure on stone is not wasted.

The next set of four projects falls into the category of 'decorative carving in the round' (see page 29). This does not mean they are all round (although most of them are); this is a term used for free-standing objects that can be seen from all sides. They are termed 'decorative' as opposed to 'figurative' in that they do not represent a living creature. Life forms do form the basis of their decoration, however, but in the shape of vegetable matter (leaves and fruit) and, in one case, a seashell.

The fine borderline between decorative and figurative carving can become a bit blurred, so it is not something you need to get hung up about. Just enjoy the next four 'decorative' carvings and the following four 'figurative' carvings. They all result in beautiful objects for your home and garden.

OAK LEAF CANDLE STAND

There are three mainstays of the decorative carver's repertoire: the acanthus leaf, the grapevine and the oak leaf. The first two originate from the Mediterranean world and are associated mainly with Classical styles. The mighty oak, although it occurs throughout the northern hemisphere, is associated more with the Gothic styles of the higher latitudes of Europe – in particular the British Isles.

It is easy to see why the oak leaf, with its attendant acorns and galls, features so strongly in English Gothic. In medieval times, the land was heavily forested with broad-leaved trees, and the mighty oak was the king of trees. Its long-lasting timber formed the structural framework of most buildings from the earliest times until the mass planting and import of softwoods displaced it in the late 19th century.

Woodcarvers, especially those working on churches and grand buildings, would mainly be carving in oak, so it is not surprising that this formed the inspiration for their designs. Stone carving cannot take its decorative inspiration from the stone itself, as stone has no form, so stone carvers used the same decorative repertoire as woodcarvers (and frequently worked in both mediums). This design is one I have made up myself, but it is inspired by medieval and Victorian Gothic oak-leaf patterns.

The idea for a candle stand (it is too thick to be called a candlestick) came about after my local stone supplier, who is generous and helpful, gave me a small off-cut of stone free of charge. I'm not one to turn down free stone, but I struggled to find a project for a block of Caen stone 5in (125mm) square by 6in (150mm) high. Eventually, I decided that a candle stand for a thick 'church' candle would make an attractive decorative object that could be used indoors or out.

I'm glad I was prompted into creating this small intricate piece, as it is an enjoyable exercise in small-scale carving in stone. But because it is small, the usual gravity-based work-holding method will not suffice. The best way of securing the piece is in a bench vice; if you don't have one, the next best option is to make up a wooden cradle and secure that to the bench.

TOOLS

1½lb (655g) dummy mallet • 2½lb (1175g) club hammer • marble point/punch • ¾in (20mm) claw chisel • ³⁄₁₆in (4mm) chisel • ¼in (6mm) chisel • ½in (13mm) chisel • ¾in (20mm) chisel • ¼in (6mm) gouge • ½in (13mm) gouge • ¾in (20mm) gouge • stone rasp • rotary burr tool (optional)

MATERIALS

Limestone block 5in (125mm) square by 6in (150mm) high

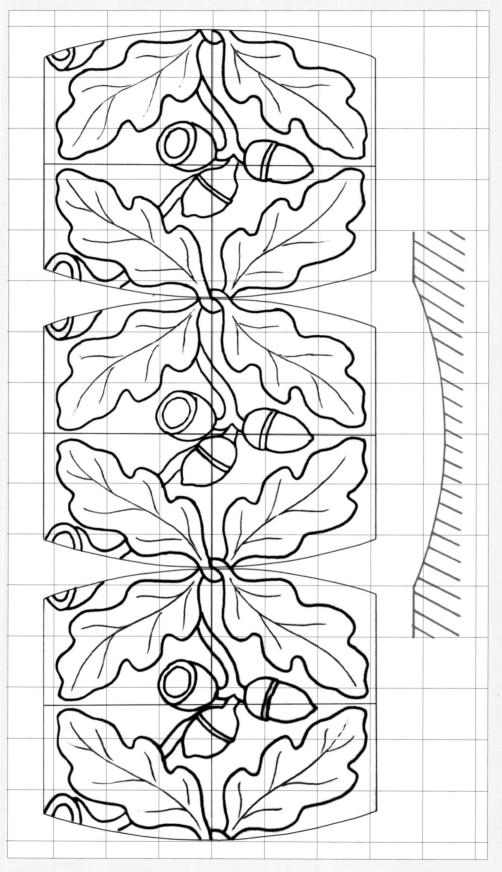

Scale drawing on a 1in (25mm) grid. Enlarge drawing to the required size (see page 10).

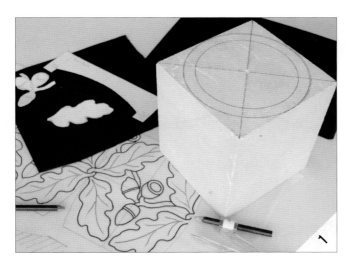

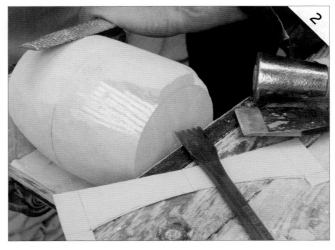

PREPARATIONS

1 Get a block of limestone 5in (125mm) square by 6in (150mm) high. Make a full-size copy of the drawing (the drawing shows the three identical sections as they wrap around the barrel shape of the piece, but you only really need one section). Trace and cut out templates of the barrel profile (shown in green on the drawing), the acorn cluster, and the oak leaf (all the leaves are the same – they are just reversed on opposite sides). Mark the centre of the 5in (125mm) square and draw circles of 5in (125mm) and 4in (100mm) diameter at each end.

ROUGHING OUT

2 Use a bench vice to hold the work, or make a wooden cradle. Use a claw chisel and bolster to work the stone down to an accurate 5in (125mm) cylinder, using a steel rule lined up to the circles at the ends. Then work the stone into a barrel shape up to the 4in (100mm) circle using the barrel template to get it even all the way round. A stone rasp is a good tool for finishing off to an even shape and a smooth surface.

3 Measure round the circumference in the middle with a fabric tape measure and divide it into six equal segments of about 2¼in (55mm) each. Draw lines from end to end at these points. Use the templates to draw on the oak leaves (reversed on opposite sides) and acorn clusters using alternate segment lines as your guide. Finish off the details by referring to the drawing. Draw a 3in (75mm) circle at each end to mark where the background will come to.

4 Block out the background to a depth of about ½in (13mm) where the pattern will allow. Work up to the 3in (75mm) circle at the ends, and try to maintain the barrel shape in the background. With any carving on a convex surface, as you carve in towards the centre the effective circumference of your background becomes smaller and the pattern elements get closer together.

CARVING THE DETAIL

5 Put a curl into the oak leaves, mainly using a ¾in (20mm) gouge. Cut the leaf lower beside the acorns so they stand out more. Use the full ½in (13mm) depth of the leaf to create a natural and lively rise and fall. Curl the leaves inwards at the top of the piece and outwards at the bottom; this gives a better visual balance when it is standing up. Make sure the level of the leaf at the stem end relates to the 'over and under' twist of the stems.

6 Shape the acorns and work their stems down to the required level. Pay particular attention to the angle at which the acorns lay with their tips in the foreground and the stem end towards the background. The empty cups are angled steeply towards the foreground.

7 Hollow out the acorn cups very carefully as they can easily break (causing you to revise the design – you can't glue stone back together as easily as you can with wood). 'Drill' into the cup by very gently tapping and simultaneously rotating a ¼in (6mm) chisel or gouge directly into the intended hollow. Open out the hole with a small gouge and, if you have one, use a rotary burr tool to create a smooth surface in the hollow.

8 Refine the shape of the acorns and their cups, and finish them by scoring a diaper pattern of contra-rotating spirals on the cups with the points of a small chisel.

9 Now return to the 12 oak leaves to carve in the detail. Create thin ridges for the veins by scooping out hollows either side of them with a small gouge, and give a twisting, curling flow to the leaves. Refine the indentations in the edges of the leaves, and use the ¼in (6mm) gouge upside down to create the over-and-under twist in the stems where they cross over at the leaf joins.

10 Undercut the edges of the leaves and acorns and tidy up the background to a smooth surface. Be careful not to break anything off at this stage, but try to make the leaves and acorns appear detached from the background.

FINISHING

11 Wrap something soft around the carving so you can stand the piece upright in the vice without damaging it. Work the surface of the 'candle platform' down about ¼in (6mm) below its original level so it is framed by the tops of the leaves and acorns. Check it is flat and level so the candle will stand upright.

12 Wash off all the dust, tidy up any uneven carving in the detail or background, and the job is finished. The candle stand and its candle will be happy indoors or out.

109

CLASSICAL VASE FINIAL

Many thousands of years ago, people started decorating the vessels they used for cooking and storage. Gradually, the decoration became more elaborate until the vessel became an entirely decorative object, the ghost of its original purpose reflected only in its general shape. Lots of the decorative vases carved in stone by the ancient Greeks and Romans were hollow vessels, some with removable lids, but in many cases any pretence of practical use was abandoned entirely. This project is an example of this type: the solid vase or urn.

The solid vase was used mainly as a finial, placed at the top of a pediment, along a balustrade or on top of a gatepost or entrance arch. It could also be found on raised plinths either side of a doorway, at the end of a vista or along a garden walk. The skyline of many a classical building is enlivened by rows of classical vases pointing skywards. This effect was employed extensively by the ancient Romans, and also in the Classical Revival styles of the 17th to the 19th centuries.

This example is a design I have put together using typical classical forms: a decoration of 'fabric' swags and tassels on a typical semi-elliptical vase with a circular foot, a false lid and a simple finial at the top (yes, the finial vase has its own finial to bring it to a point). I have kept the decoration fairly simple in a 'Greek Revival' style so as not to overload it with detail.

Every carving has its own particular challenges; in this case, the challenge lies in creating the vase shape. With a geometrical shape such as a circle, it is fairly easy for a casual observer to see any defects in the shape. As a woodturner, I am conscious how easy it would be if you could use a lathe, but stone lathes are semi-industrial machines that a hobby carver is unlikely to have, so we have to employ a lot of tricks with templates and compasses to make sure the vase looks properly round.

This is a fairly small-scale vase for home or garden display, but you will need to make it larger (see page 10) if you want it as a finial for a substantial gate pier.

TOOLS

1½lb (655g) dummy mallet • 2½lb (1175g) club hammer • marble point/ punch • ¾in (20mm) claw chisel • 2in (50mm) bolster/pitcher • ³⁄₁₆in (4mm) chisel • ¼in (6mm) chisel • ½in (13mm) chisel • ¾in (20mm) chisel • ¼in (6mm) gouge • ½in (13mm) gouge • ¾in (20mm) gouge • stone rasp • angle grinder or stone/concrete saw (optional)

MATERIALS

Limestone block 8in (200mm) square by 10in (250mm) high

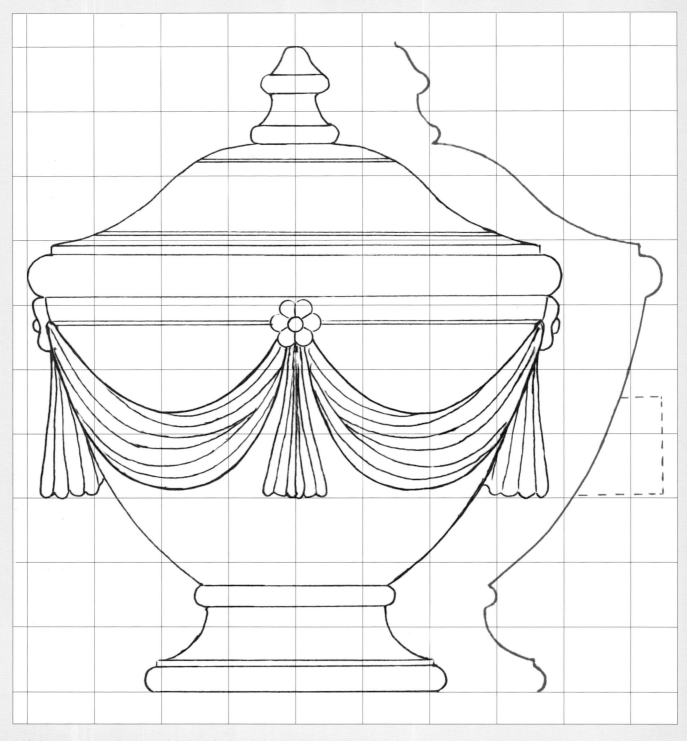

Scale drawing on a 1in (25mm) grid. Enlarge drawing to the required size (see page 10).

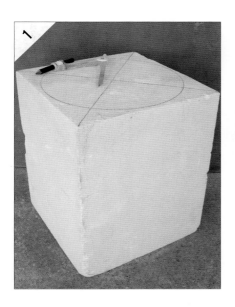

PREPARATIONS

1 Get a block of limestone 8in (200mm) square x 10in (250mm) high. Mark the centres of the 8in (200mm) square ends with a point so you can find them again later, and draw circles of 8in (200mm) diameter at each end.

2 Make an accurate full-size copy of the drawing (you will need to measure heights and diameters off this). Trace and accurately cut out at least two templates of the vase profile (shown in green on the drawing); you will need to cut them up later. Also carefully cut out a hollow template for an 8in (200mm) circle and all the other bead diameters. Get some callipers that will expand up to 8in (200mm).

3 Make up a 'cradle' out of scrap wood to hold the stone on its side while you work on the rounded sides. It should be a bit longer than the stone and have a 90-degree V 'trough'. It must be strong enough to withstand the hammering as you rough out the stone, so use screws rather than nails when you assemble it. It is best fixed to a board that can be screwed or clamped to the banker. Also cut a few wedges; you will need these to support the vase later as the ends are cut away.

ROUGHING OUT

4 Lay the stone on its side in the cradle to rough it into an 8in (200mm)-diameter cylinder. Working with the point, claw chisel and bolster, remove the square corners and work the stone down level with the circles marked at the ends. Keep checking with a steel rule until the surface is completely level from the top circle to the corresponding point on the bottom circle. You can use a rasp to achieve a smooth surface to make sure there is no pitting where the widest bead will be.

5 Stand the stone upright and draw a 1¼in (30mm) circle at the top end using the centre marked at the start. Draw a circumference line 8½in (215mm) up from the base (we measure from the base as we lose the top measuring points as we work) and another line 6⅞in (175mm) from the base. Carefully remove the stone outside the upper circle to leave the stone that will form the finial of the vase, then work down and outwards to the lower of the two lines to produce a dome shape that will leave enough stone to form the 'lid' of the vase. The finial has the potential to break off and wreck the job if you are too rough with it, so proceed carefully.

CARVING THE FINIAL AND 'LID'

6 Before carving the finial it is best to finish shaping the 'lid' while we still have our original centre point to use as a datum. Using compasses with the pencil extended, draw and redraw a series of concentric circles around the lid surface. Used in conjunction with the profile template, these circles help you see where stone needs to be removed to make the surface the same all the way round.

7 Work the lid surface down to its final shape with chisels and gouges, then smooth it off with the rasp. Keep redrawing the concentric circles and checking with the profile template until it is just right.

8 While the top centre point is still there, use it to draw circles for the upper and lower V lines and also the edge fillet for the lid. Use a ¼in (6mm) chisel to cut the V lines as neatly as you can, and to cut a clean vertical fillet around the outer edge. It is important to make a neat job of the circle on the outer edge, as it is easy to see if it is not right.

9 Now very carefully shape the lower and upper beads on the finial. Use small circle templates and a profile template to check that both beads are circular and the right size before shaping the top and the waist. All the shaping can be done with the rasp to avoid the risk of breaking the finial under the chisel, then carefully finish off the surface with the ½in (13mm) gouge.

CARVING THE CENTRAL SECTION

10 Measuring off the drawing, mark out the circumference lines for the central bead and the swags and drapes below it. Use a fabric tape measure to divide the circumference into four equal sections, and draw the 'tassels' at these points. Draw in the swags between them, making sure their upper and lower edges are all on the same level and reach the lowest point of their curve exactly between the tassels. Now chisel round the centre bead line and the edges of the swags.

11 With the piece laid back in the cradle, work the centre bead into a *torus* (bull-nose) profile using the ¾in (20mm) gouge and the rasp. Now carefully shape the side of the vase between the bead and the swag, using part of the cardboard template to get the right degree of curve down towards the bottom of the vase.

ROUGHING OUT AND CARVING THE BASE

12 Start the base by drawing a 4½in (115mm)-diameter circle using the centre point you marked at the beginning. Next, draw a circumference line under the swags and tassels 3in (75mm) up from the base. We now have to remove a fair amount of stone. Using an angle grinder to cut up the stone can reduce the amount of chiselling, but take care not to go too deep with your cuts.

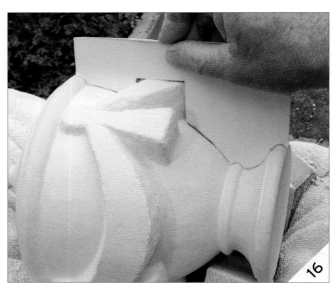

13 Chisel neatly round the base circle. Remove the bulk of the stone, sloping from a depth of 1in (25mm) at the circumference line and working down to the base circle.

14 Chisel a deep V for the neck of the foot, measuring from the drawing. To get this V circular and to the right depth, it helps to make up this simple jig. Get a strip of wood and screw a screw through it so it protrudes ⅝in (15mm). Fix a stop under the strip of wood 1½in (40mm) back from the screw. Place the wood on the circumference of the foot, with the stop against the underside. When the screw touches the bottom of the V, with the wood parallel to the axis of the vase, the V is at the right depth.

15 Using gouges and a rasp, form the cavetto moulding and two beads for the foot. Use the side profile template to check the shape of the mouldings, and a circle template cut in two to check that the neck bead is circular and the right diameter.

FINISHING THE VASE AND SWAGS

16 Remove the surplus stone under the swags and tassels, and shape the sides of the vase to give a smooth flow from the main centre bead down to the neck of the foot. Use the side profile template with a section cut out where the swag interrupts the line. You need to get it so the smooth curve follows through this interruption as though the swag is laid over the vase.

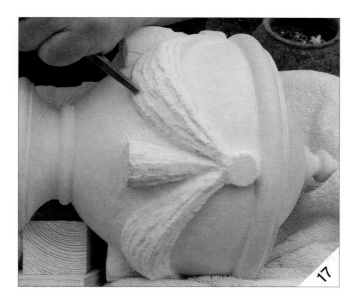

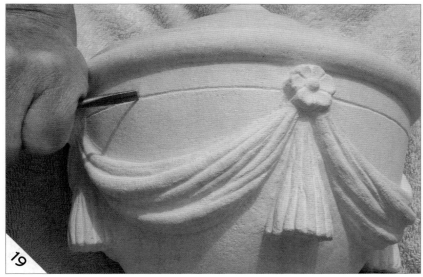

17 Reduce the thickness of the swags so they flow smoothly around the sides of the vase. They need to have a thickness of about ¼in (6mm) at the edges and about ⅝in (15mm) in the middle so they appear to hang naturally under the influence of gravity. Shape the tassels so their lower ends seem to hang slightly outwards as they fall.

18 Mainly using a ¼in (6mm) gouge, form the folds of the drapery. Take a look at how real fabrics hang and try to capture that feel. The folds tend to cross over a little at various points. Form the tassels into cords converging at the top, and undercut around the bottom so the tassel appears round. Carefully carve the little flowers that everything hangs from, using the same gouge to form the six petals and the stamen and a chisel to separate the petals.

19 Undercut round the edges of the drapery so it appears detached from the vase. Tidy up the line of the vase so the curve follows cleanly through from one side of the swag to the other. Carve a V-line around the circumference, level with the centre of the flowers, matching the lines in the lid.

20 Finally, tidy up any uneven carving in the detail or background, and finish off the vase surface with 120-grit abrasive to give a good smooth finish. Leave the swags, tassels and flowers with their 'off the tools' finish. Carefully wash off all the dust, and the job is finished.

GRAPE LEAF BOWL

There is something about grapes that touches the human psyche. Perhaps it is the association with fruitful abundance, health-restoring nourishment (we traditionally take grapes when visiting sick people) and the heady pleasures of wine. Little wonder that they have been used abundantly from Classical Greek and Roman times to the present day to embellish carved, moulded, painted and printed surfaces.

The grapevine relies for its decorative effect on four elements: the cloud-like billows of the grapes, the large indented five-pointed leaves with their deep 'eyes', the little curling twists of the tendrils, and the rough spiralling bark of the sinuous vines.

We first saw the grapevine as a rocky ruin in project 6. Now we see it in a more complex form with this ornamental bowl. It is a design I have put together myself, inspired by the richness, depth and naturalism of the Baroque style. It is based around a large single leaf, supported by a circle of twisting vine, with bunches of grapes tumbling over the inside and outside of the bowl. It is designed to capture a spirit of fruitful abundance.

Bowls have long been used not only as utilitarian vessels, but also for purely decorative purposes. The precedent is well established in ceramics, silverware and woodturning. Strangely,

it is less often encountered in woodcarving, but stone carvers frequently use decorative hollow forms despite the difficulty of hollowing stone vessels. This carving makes a small concession to the utilitarian function of a bowl in that items can be placed in it (such as ornamental soaps if used in a bathroom), but its primary function is to please the eye.

I don't know how thin you can make a stone bowl before it shatters, and I have no wish to find out on the last tap of the chisel at the end of a complex carving. The stone must not only survive the carving process, but must also survive many years of being moved around. For this reason, I have kept the design on the 'chunky' side, with the bowl walls reinforced by the bunches of grapes, tendrils and thick vines. I have used the carver's trick of making the edges fairly thin but increasing the thickness rapidly as you move away from the edge.

TOOLS

1½lb (655g) dummy mallet • 2½lb (1175g) club hammer • marble point/punch • ¾in (20mm) claw chisel • 2in (50mm) bolster/pitcher • ³⁄₁₆in (4mm) chisel • ¼in (6mm) chisel • ½in (13mm) chisel • ¾in (20mm) chisel • ¼in (6mm) gouge • ½in (13mm) gouge • ¾in (20mm) gouge • stone rasp • stone/concrete saw (optional)

MATERIALS

Limestone block 10in (250mm) square by 5in (125mm) high

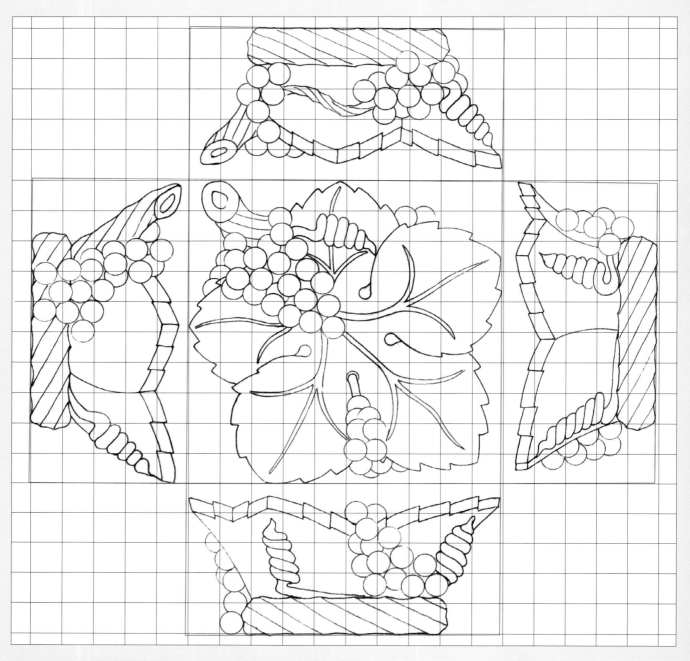

Scale drawing on a 1in (25mm) grid. Enlarge drawing to the required size (see page 10).

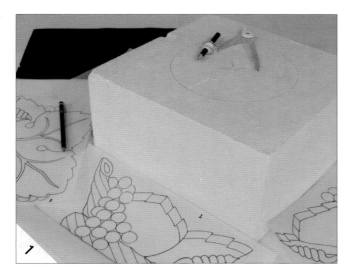

PREPARATIONS

1 Get a block of limestone 10in (250mm) square by 5in (125mm) high. Make a full-size copy of the drawing, including the side profiles. Mark the centre of the underside and draw a circle 7in (180mm) diameter. You will use this circle when you come to do the base later, but a pencil mark will wear away before you get to it, so scratch it in with a point.

2 Trace the pattern onto the top, then trace on the side profiles, taking care to match up the correct sides in relation to the top.

ROUGHING OUT THE UPPER PARTS

3 Because this project is a complex three-dimensional piece that is hollowed and undercut, roughing out the shape is a large part of the job. Start by cutting out the spare material that

is outside the pattern outline on the top and sides. If you cut a square edge against the horizontal and vertical outlines, the angle where they meet will roughly be where the edges of the leaves will be. How much surplus you have at the top will depend on the thickness of your stone.

4 There is no denying that hollowing a block of stone is hard and tedious work. It is best to hollow the inside while there is still a full block of stone on the outside. A bowl shape is a bit like an upside-down dome – it can withstand a lot of pressure from the outside inwards, but not so much from the inside outwards. Drill a series of holes in the centre so the stone has somewhere to break into (make sure you don't go too deep), then chip away towards the centre with a small-ended chisel. As the hole gets bigger you can switch to a claw chisel. For this piece, work around the grape clusters and tendril, leaving them untouched for now.

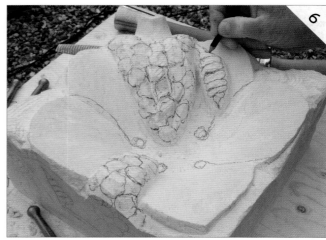

5 Cut the leaf edges down to their correct level. Open out the inside of the bowl until it is about 3in (75mm) deep. Finish the basic shaping of the inside with a ¾in (20mm) gouge and a rasp.

6 Form the overall shape of the grape bunches, the tendril and the stem. Each grape will be about ¾in (20mm) in diameter, so make sure the bunch has sufficient bulk to accommodate enough whole grapes. Note how the grapes flow over the edge of the bowl and leave enough thickness above the leaf to accommodate this. Redraw the detail before you proceed to carving.

CARVING THE DETAIL ON THE UPPER PARTS

7 It is best to complete the detail on the inside of the bowl while it still has its full structural strength. Form the individual grapes (as we did in project 6) by separating them into layers with a small chisel and rounding them over with the inside of the ¾in (20mm) gouge. Try to get a natural-looking fall and flow, especially where they tumble over the edges of the bowl. To separate the grapes neatly you need to sharpen up the little triangular hollows where the spheres meet. The best way to do this is by grinding a wood chisel to a sharp point and pushing it into the hollow.

8 Carve the small tendril, and shape the end of the main stem. Carefully carve a hollow for the pith at the end of the stem, and carve the spiralling bark around it as we did in project 6. Create a few smaller stems coming off the main stem, including one leading to the tendril, as they disappear into the grapes.

9 The five segments of the leaf have 'eyes' where they meet and overlap in the middle. One of the eyes has a grape stem coming out of it. Drill out the three eyes that are clear with a ⅜in (10mm) masonry drill, going right through to the underside so the bowl can drain when outside in the rain (always a consideration for hollow forms). Carve an overlap on the leaves running down into the eyes. Remove some surplus stone on the outer edge (a saw is best on the corners to reduce the risk of breaking the points off) and carve indentations along the leaf edge.

10 Finish the detail on the leaves by carving raised veins with the inside of a ¼in (6mm) gouge. Use larger gouges to make hollows between the veins and create a natural flow and curl to the leaf surface. The leaf is a major element of the design, so try to get a good finish.

ROUGHING OUT THE SIDES

11 With the upper part of the bowl finished, we are back to some heavy roughing out on the outside. To reduce the risk of breaking off the ends of the leaves as they get thinner, it is best to use a saw to remove the bulk. Make up a wooden 'cradle' that will tilt the bowl at an angle of about 30 degrees so you can work on the sides.

12 Carefully remove surplus stone from the sides of the bowl with a small chisel, avoiding heavy impacts. Work back to the ring of vine stem that encircles the underside and acts as a base. Use the 7in (180mm)-diameter circle we marked at the start as your guide on the underside, but allow the vine to extend into an oval at the stem end and the leaf point opposite. Leave stone on the sides for the grapes and tendrils. The leaf edges can be worked to a thickness of about ½in (13mm) – the rasp is the best tool to use near the edges – but increase the thickness as you move away from the edges so that most of the bowl wall is at least 1in (25mm) thick.

RINGING TONES

You will notice an interesting phenomenon when you carve a hollow form. As the sides get thinner you will hear a distinct alteration in the tone as you strike the chisel, changing from a dull tap into a resonant metallic ring. In theory this tone should suddenly become dull again if a crack develops, but let's hope we never find out!

CARVING THE DETAIL ON THE SIDES

13 Form the grapes on the sides of the bowl in the same way as we did at the top. Make them tumble naturally down the sides as though hanging in a bunch. The grapes at the edges of the bunch must wrap in towards the bowl wall. Some grapes fall right down to the 'ground' level outside the vine base.

14 Put some more pieces of board under the wooden cradle to increase the working angle to about 45 degrees. This will help you work under the leaf points. Carve the tendrils under the leaf points, using a ¼in (6mm) chisel and the inside of a ½in (13mm) gouge. As well as being decorative, these also give some support to the bowl wall where the leaf points project. Merge the stem of the tendril into the encircling vine of the base.

15 Finally, carve the spiralling bark on the vine that encircles the base. The vine should be about 1¼in (30mm) thick and should appear to connect to the main stem and the thinner stems and tendrils. Mould it into the bottom of the bowl so it appears to support the whole piece.

FINISHING

16 The grapes can be given a light rubbing with abrasive to give them a smooth round finish. The leaves and stems are best left 'off the tools'. These photos illustrate how it should look from the top and all sides; use them as a reference when you are carving the detail.

17 Wash off all the dust, tidy up any uneven carving exposed by the washing, and the job is finished. The bowl will be happy indoors or out. The drainage holes in the 'eyes' of the leaves will make sure it doesn't fill up with water.

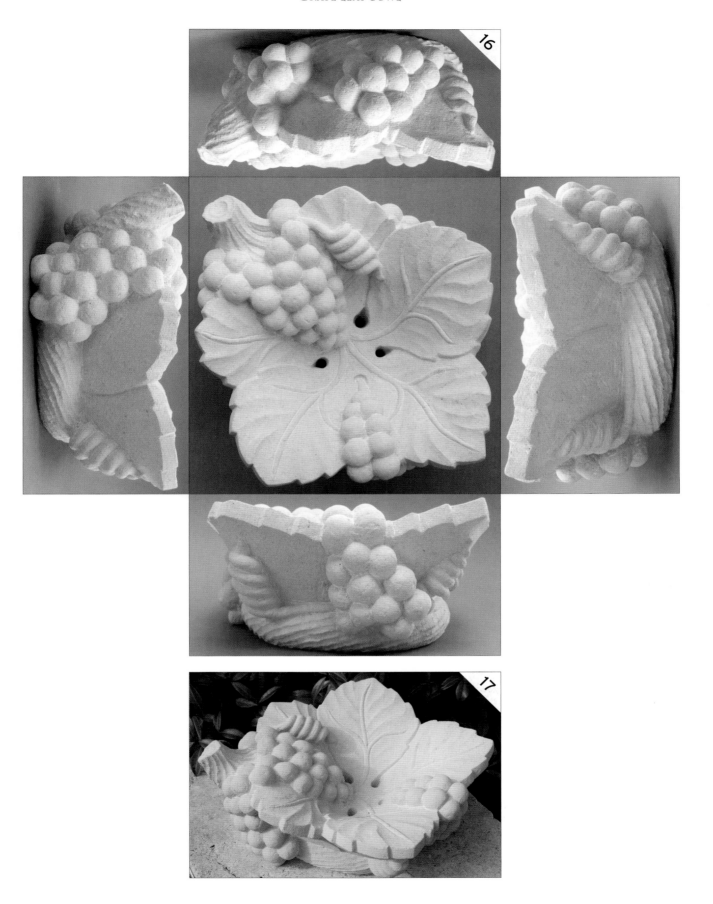

SHELL DISH

Ancient Greece was a land of coast and islands, so it is not surprising that seashells figure prominently in the decorative vocabulary of the Classical styles. The scallop shell, in particular, appears widely among niches, cornices, pediments and fountains. This precedent was carried through to the Roman period and on to the Classical Revival styles from the 16th century onwards. Botticelli's Venus famously emerges enticingly from a giant scallop shell.

Shells do not figure much in the Gothic style, so they remain very much a Classical motif, complete with a volute scroll at the 'hinge' end of the shell. This example is adapted from a design in the *Handbook of Ornament* (Franz Meyer, 1888, currently published by Dover Publications).

The whole piece is formed around a circle 15in (380mm) diameter, with a height of 6in (152mm) to the top of the scroll. It is a fairly shallow bowl form with an overall wall thickness of around 2in (50mm), so there is much 'roughing out' involved to remove about two-thirds of the original stone block. The finished carving is a reasonable weight to lift, but the original block weighs around 117lb (53kg), so unless you are very fit and strong I would advise you to use lifting gear to lift the block onto the banker.

Because there is so much stone to remove, and hollowing is tedious work, I used the angle grinder more in this project than in any of the previous ones. This is optional, as this tool creates a large amount of dust that spreads over everything in the vicinity, but it does reduce the amount of hammering you have to do. Just remember to take special care to control the tool for your own safety and to avoid wrecking the job with a cut that is too deep.

This shell dish will look great on its own in your garden (or even in your house), but it will look even better if, when you have developed the skills and confidence, you tackle the dolphin pedestal in project 18. I have designed both pieces to work in combination, provided you make them both to the same scale as shown in the drawings. But one step at a time.... Carve the shell dish first, then look forward to setting it on the dolphin pedestal when you are ready for it.

TOOLS
1½lb (655g) dummy mallet • 2½lb (1175g) club hammer • marble point/punch • ¾in (20mm) claw chisel • 2in (50mm) bolster/pitcher • ³⁄₁₆in (4mm) chisel • ¼in (6mm) chisel • ½in (13mm) chisel • ¾in (20mm) chisel • ¼in (6mm) gouge • ½in (13mm) gouge • ¾in (20mm) gouge • stone rasp • angle grinder (optional)

MATERIALS
Limestone block 15in (380mm) square by 6in (150mm) high
Weight approx. 117lb (53kg) – use lifting gear

Scale drawing on a 1in (25mm) grid. Enlarge drawing to the required size (see page 10).

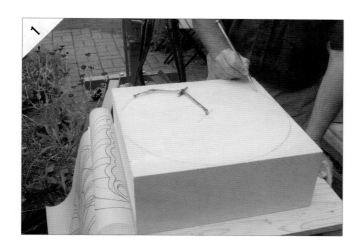

PREPARATIONS

1 Get a block of limestone 15in (380mm) square by 6in (150mm) high. **Weight warning: this will weigh about 117lb (53kg), so lifting gear is recommended.** Make a full-size copy of the drawing. Mark the centres of the top and underside and draw circles 15in (380mm) in diameter. A pencil mark will wear away before you have finished with it, so scratch in the circles and centres with a point.

ROUGHING OUT

2 Make a cradle (similar to the grapevine bowl cradle but bigger and stronger) to support the piece at an angle of about 30 degrees so you can work on the sides and see the underside circle. Use a point, claw and bolster to remove the corners (you can cut them up with an angle grinder first to speed up the process) and create a 15in (380mm)-diameter circular 'cheese' of stone. This doesn't need to be as perfect as the classical vase, but work it to a reasonable accuracy.

3 Take the full-size copy of the drawing and trace the scroll pattern onto one end of the top surface. Holding the drawing in place, mark the ends of each of the flat and concave segments of the shell around the edge of the stone (it is not worth tracing them on as they will be removed in the roughing out). Use a set square to draw these lines vertically at least 2in (50mm) down the sides. Refer to the drawing of the side profile for guidance, and draw what will be the top edge of the dish. It starts 5in (125mm) above the base level at the front, falling gradually to 4in (100mm) above the base just in front of the scroll.

4 Remove the surplus stone above the rim of the dish, leaving the scroll section untouched, then start hollowing the bowl. An angle grinder is very messy and dusty, but it will greatly speed up this process if you cut the stone into strips and cubes before chiselling with the point and claw. Remember that an angle grinder must be used with care or it can quickly wreck the job (and you!).

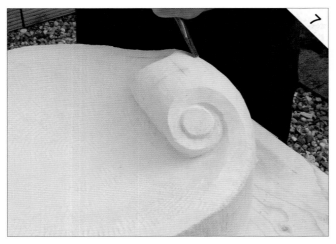

5 Make a template from stiff card or MDF for the inner profile of the bowl. This is shown in green on the drawing and is aligned on the axis from the front to the scroll end. Chisel down with the claw until the template fits accurately when standing on the table surface. This will ensure that you have 2in (50mm) of stone left at the base of the bowl.

6 Continue shaping the bowl until you have formed a smooth shape for the inside of the shell, working from the level established by the template. The bowl is deepest at the end nearest the scroll. You will need to start forming the area around the scroll to finish the bowl.

7 Form the outline of the scroll into the familiar 'Swiss Roll' volute. Mark the centreline of the scroll and always measure from this to ensure that each side is symmetrical. Curve the scroll down to the sides of the dish. You will need to refine this line later.

CARVING INSIDE THE SHELL

8 By referring to the drawing, and the lines you marked on the stone in step 3, draw in the shell segments and the two horseshoe-shaped rings. Make sure everything is set out accurately, as these lines will define the key features of the shell. Mark the lines with a chisel, as the pencil will disappear as you work. Also mark which segments are flat and which are concave, dropping the concave ends ½in (13mm) below the flat edges.

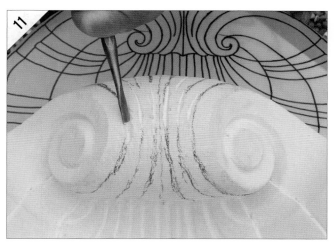

9 Carve out the concave segments with gouges and the flat segments with chisels, making sure you obtain smooth surfaces and clean sharp edges. It is the sharpness of these edges that will distinguish your shell dish from the moulded concrete versions in the garden centre. Pay particular attention to the point at which each segment meets the horseshoe-shaped rings; these rings form a ⅛in (3mm) step with the vertical edge facing outwards. This step follows across the flats and into the hollows all the way round. This affects the width of the flat segment; the inner flat has to extend sideways beyond the outer flat to form a step into the concave segment (you will see what I mean when you try it).

10 To finish the inside of the shell, mark out and cut in the narrow channels that divide the flat segments in two. These also have to be stepped where they meet the horseshoe rings. These channels are formed only on the outer two rings of flats. The innermost part of the shell is already formed of narrow flats and channels too small to be subdivided.

CARVING THE SCROLL

11 Carefully mark out the elements of the scroll by referring to the drawing and finished photos. Measure out from the centreline to make sure each element is symmetrical, and make sure each line has a smooth curve and flow. Chisel in the lines so you don't lose them as you work.

12 Carefully carve the scroll, making sure you get clean, crisp lines on the volutes at each end. The central moulding is a shallow inverted V, and either side of it there are convex curving mouldings flowing down to the bowl and over to the back. Notice how the volutes slope at an angle, so you need to reduce the stone in the middle of the scroll by about ⅜in (10mm) below its original level. The scroll is a defining feature of the carving, so take your time and get it right.

CARVING THE SIDES AND BASE

13 Turn the piece upside down on a soft surface to protect the carved areas. Draw a circle 8in (200mm) in diameter on the underside, with its centre 1in (25mm) behind the centre of the whole piece (in the direction of the scroll). This will offset the base moulding towards the scroll end, giving a better visual balance to the finished piece. Inscribe the circle with a point so you don't lose it.

14 Mark a line around the edge of the shell 1½in (40mm) below the top edge of the flats. Make another mark on top of the flats ⅜in (10mm) in from the edge at the front, reducing to ¼in (6mm) on the segment nearest the scroll. Now chisel in to the top line and slope down to the lower line so you form an edge for the shell segments that is almost a right angle. Use the rasp to work the ends of the concave segments into the same smooth line. This will provide the basis for the edge of the dish.

15 Put the piece back in the cradle so you can work on the underside. Remove the stone in a gentle curve from the line you just made below the top edge down to the base circle, keeping around 2in (50mm) thickness of stone. The piece is getting potentially more fragile, so don't go smashing away at it. Use a saw to cut away under the top edge, and chip away the remaining rock with a small chisel (this exerts less pressure than a large tool). Work sideways rather than directly up or down to reduce the risk of breaking off more than you intended.

16 Mark a line around the outside of the bowl ¾in (20mm) below the top, following the line of the flats and concave channels. Draw lines on the underside of the dish to correspond roughly with the channels in the bowl. Now cut channels in the underside to reflect the flats and curves on the top, increasing the thickness of the stone as you move away from the edge. These channels are a significant feature when the carving is viewed from the side, so work them to a good finish.

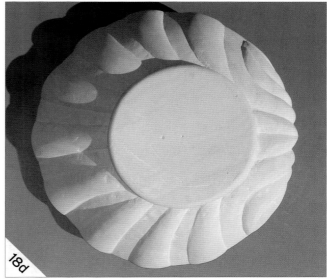

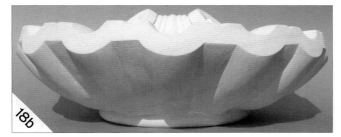

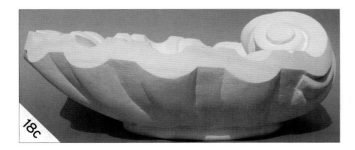

17 Finally, work the base circle into a ¾in (20mm) thick *torus* moulding, using the rasp and the ¾in (20mm) gouge. You can work with the piece placed carefully upside down on a soft surface provided you don't hammer too hard. Use pieces of board to support the whole edge of the dish and the scroll so you don't break the piece in half.

FINISHING

18 Wash off all the dust, tidy up any uneven carving exposed by the washing, and the job is finished. This dish has no drainage hole as it would spoil the carving, so it should be used as a birdbath, or even as part of a fountain. These images illustrate how it should look from above, below and the sides; use them for reference when you are carving the detail.

133

PART 4

Figure sculptures

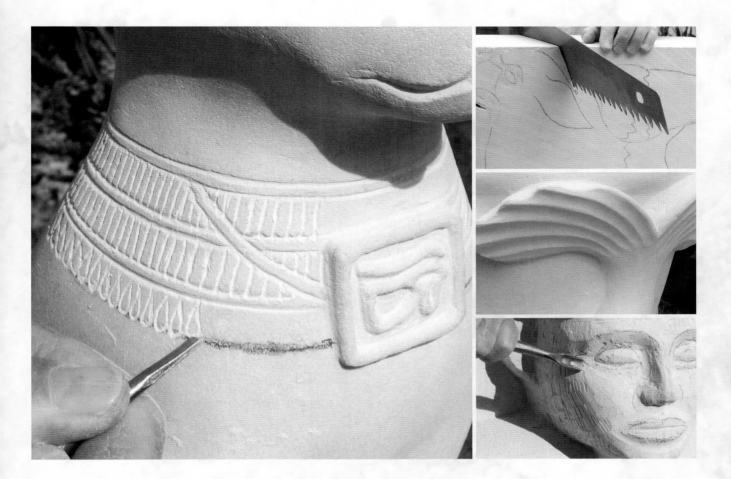

FOR MANY PEOPLE, MYSELF INCLUDED, figure sculpture is the most difficult form of carving. The slightest alteration in a feature can completely alter the expression of a face or the 'body language' of a figure. In a carving of an animal, human or bird, most observers will know what it should look like and can spot a poor likeness when they see one. This is less of a problem with decorative carving, as the observer is less likely to know what shape the pattern should have been so long as it looks pleasing.

These last four projects do not require you to reach the sculptural standards of Canova or Michelangelo. I have kept them to a standard achievable by an amateur of moderate experience and ability (after all, I have to be able to make them myself to show you). As three-dimensional free-standing objects, much of the carving time is spent working the stone to the form of the figure with proportionally less time spent on detail.

I have set out to produce figures that are not like the moulded concrete statues you can buy cheaply in garden centres. I'm not criticizing these products, as many of them are very attractive, but because they are mass-produced you don't want your painstakingly hand-carved pieces to be mistaken for them. You want people to notice your figures because they are unusual, and then examine them more closely to see that they are the real deal.

To keep the weight and cost of stone at manageable levels, I have kept the figures moderate in size. If you want to make them bigger, just expand the drawing to a larger size (see page 10). Because the figures are not large, most of them will benefit from being mounted on a plinth, or a display wall specially constructed with platforms at different levels to accommodate several objects. Good-quality concrete or composite blocks, built up and painted in white or cream, will set off your carvings to advantage. If you can master figure carving to a good standard, your horizons are limitless and you can look forward to creating many more beautiful objects of your own design and creation.

EGYPTIAN CAT

A lot of people love cats, but the Ancient Egyptians took it a bit further – they worshipped cats. No, really; I mean they literally worshipped cats. To an Ancient Egyptian, the cat was a sacred creature with connections in high places. The cat-goddess Bastet was the daughter of the sun-god Ra (top god in the Egyptian pantheon of gods) and is depicted with a host of sun-related symbolism.

This cat is based on a bronze statuette in the British Museum (around 2,500 years old), who would have been worshipped as the embodiment of Bastet. She is clearly a very pampered cat, dripping with jewellery as well as symbolism. When daddy is the sun-god, daddy's little princess gets expensive presents, even if she is just a cat. This is a cat with attitude, sitting in a majestic pose with a very superior expression.

The decorative detail is very fine and in most cases has to be 'engraved' onto the stone with the point of a small chisel. Starting at the top of the head, there is a very small symbol that I could not identify on the original, so I have substituted a simple sun-disc streaming parallel rays. The nose and earrings (made of real gold on the original) have to be carved very carefully with a small gouge.

The amulet on the chest is a small panel carved in very low relief. The 'Eye of Horus' depicted on it relates to the hawk-god Horus – a protective deity closely related with Ra, whose job in this case is to watch over Bastet (hence the 'eye') and protect her from harm.

The engraving on her chest is a sacred scarab beetle (yes, beetles can be sacred too) with the outstretched wings of a bird. Bird wings are another protective symbol associated with Ra and Horus, so a beetle with bird wings, holding a small sun-disc in its claws, is not at all strange. The engraved necklace pattern is, as far as I know, just a necklace pattern.

The Egyptian cat looks quite different to our modern domestic pet, partly because it is heavily stylized but also because it is a different species – the jungle cat (*Felis chaus*), which is slim and athletic with large ears and long legs. Modern cats have inherited the superior attitude, if not the appearance.

TOOLS

1½lb (655g) dummy mallet • 2½lb (1175g) club hammer • marble point/punch • ¾in (20mm) claw chisel • 2in (50mm) bolster/pitcher • ³⁄₁₆in (4mm) chisel • ¼in (6mm) chisel • ½in (13mm) chisel • ¾in (20mm) chisel • ¼in (6mm) gouge • ½in (13mm) gouge • ¾in (20mm) gouge • stone rasp • stone/concrete saw • coping saw with tile-cutting blade

MATERIALS

Limestone block 6 x 9in (150 x 230mm) and 18in (460mm) high **Weight approx. 84lb (40kg) – lifting gear recommended**

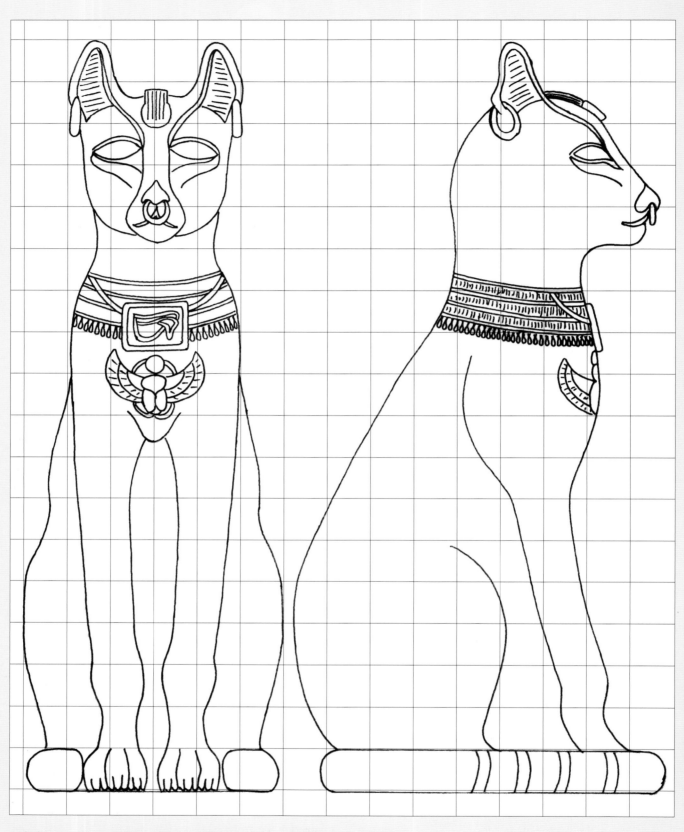

Scale drawing on a 1in (25mm) grid. Enlarge drawing to the required size (see page 10).

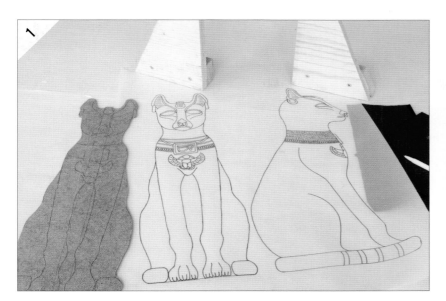

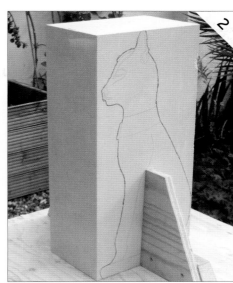

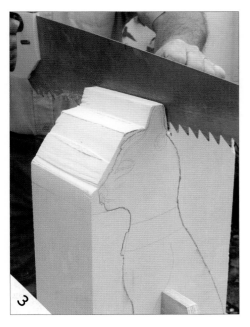

PREPARATIONS

1 Get a block of limestone 6 x 9in (150 x 230mm) and 18in (460mm) high. **Weight warning: this will weigh about 84lb (40kg) so lifting gear is recommended.** Make a full-size copy of the drawing. Trace and cut out a stiff card or hardboard template of the front profile. Also make two braces to fix on to the banker to hold the tall, thin piece of stone upright as you carve.

2 Trace the side profiles onto both sides of the stone, making sure they line up exactly. Place the stone on the banker and fix the braces in place to hold it securely.

ROUGHING OUT

3 With this carving, the ears and nose of the cat are potentially vulnerable to being damaged during roughing out, so it is best to isolate them with saw cuts at the start. As the stone is only 6in (150mm) wide, sawing is fairly easy and is the best option for removing much of the surplus stone.

4 Lay the carving on its back and rough out the front edge using point, claw and chisel. Use a rasp to work the face back to the exact line of the tracing. This will ensure the profile of your cat matches the drawing.

5 Finish the roughing out of the profile on the back edge using the saw, point, claw, chisel and rasp as before. You should now have a perfect side profile for the carving.

6 Draw a centreline down the front and back of the carving. Carefully mark out the front and back profile using the template as a guide. This is not straightforward as the face is now convoluted, so check that the measurements are the same both sides of the centreline.

7 Remove the surplus stone as before, using chisel and rasp to get an accurate front and back profile. Leave the bit at the bottom for now as we need the weight and flat sides to support the piece while we work on the head.

CARVING THE HEAD

8 Carefully round over the edges of the head and neck and work the face into shape. Refer to the finished photos as well as the drawing to see how it should be. Draw and then redraw the features of the face as you work, and keep checking against the centreline to make sure it is symmetrical. Remove the surplus stone around the earrings, nose ring, and the decorative symbol at the top. Tap gently and use the rasp whenever possible, as the head is supported on a fairly narrow neck.

9 Start the detail carving by marking the position of the eyes. Carve the narrow ridge from the inner edge of the eyes up to the ears using the inside of a ¼in (6mm) gouge. Carefully carve the eyes, which are quite deep-set and facing forward, and use the edge of the small gouge to shape the eyelids. This is very fine work and it is usually easier to gently scrape the chisel along with both hands, rather like woodcarving.

10 Gently carve the ears, including the earrings, while the stone between the ears is still in place for support. Use the points of a small chisel to scratch the 'bars' inside the ears. When the outer sides of the ears are finished, you can remove the surplus stone between them. A tile-cutting blade in a coping saw or junior hacksaw is a good way of doing this without chiselling, as the ears are now quite fragile. Finish with a rasp. Also note how the small decoration on the head is finished.

11 Carve the narrow slit of the mouth, which curves up sharply where it meets the nose (draw it in before you cut, as the slightest difference in its position completely alters the appearance). Hollow out slightly between the mouth and the eye, and refine the shape of the jaw with the rasp. Finish with 120-grit abrasive to remove the score marks of the rasp and get a good fine finish (be careful not to dull the detail with abrasives).

SHAPING THE LEGS AND BODY

12 Draw the outline of the front legs and the haunch of the rear legs. Cut out the gap between the front legs first, then remove surplus stone on the outside of the front legs and work back to the haunches.

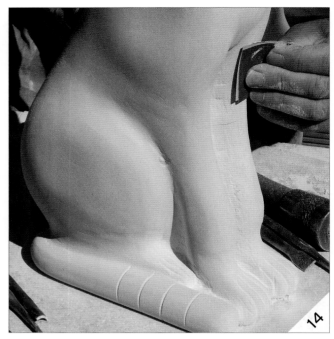

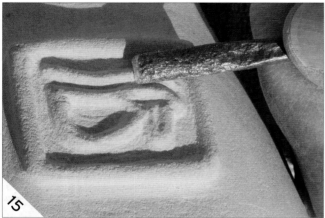

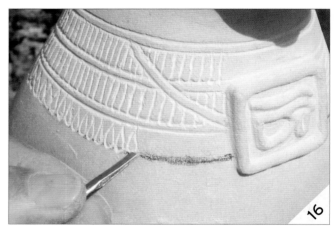

13 Round over all the square edges of the body and legs and work them into shape. Do the same with the chest, taking care to create a suitable surface for the necklace and 'winged scarab' engraving. The amulet hanging on the chest stands proud of the body surface by about ⅛in (3mm).

14 Refine the shape of the legs and feet. This takes us to the base of the carving, where we have a tail on the left side but not on the right. This requires some adjustment of the position of the back feet. Carve the detail of the toes and claws, and the striped 'bars' on the cat's tail.

FINISHING

15 Use abrasives to remove the score marks of the rasp and, in particular, create a perfect surface for the engraving of the necklace and winged scarab. Carefully carve the amulet with its small and very low relief Eye of Horus pattern. The pattern is not so much carved as 'scratched in' very carefully with the concave points of a ¼in (6mm) gouge.

16 The scratching technique is used again to engrave the very fine strands, bars and 'teardrops' on the necklace. Mark it out carefully (masking tape helps in getting the necklace line right) to make it look neat. Cut the engraving just deep enough to be visible without chewing up the surface of the neck. Scribe in the straps of the amulet first so they appear to lie over the necklace.

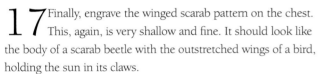

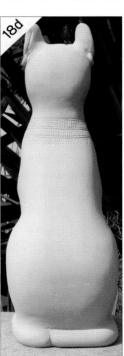

17 Finally, engrave the winged scarab pattern on the chest. This, again, is very shallow and fine. It should look like the body of a scarab beetle with the outstretched wings of a bird, holding the sun in its claws.

18 Wash off all the dust, and your Egyptian cat is ready to stand in your home or garden, and worship if you feel so inclined. These photos illustrate how it should look from the front, back and sides; use them as a reference when you are carving the detail.

Project 16

EGYPTIAN HEAD

There are many periods in history when it has been fashionable to have a beard (for men at least – they never really caught on with women), but as far as I know there is only one time and place when false beards were fashionable: Ancient Egypt. Three thousand years ago, no self-respecting pharaoh would be seen dead without a long cylindrical mass of someone else's hair stuck on the end of his chin. Being seen dead was, of course, an important consideration in the Ancient Egyptian religion, with its emphasis on the afterlife.

This project is adapted from a statue of Thutmose III (1479–1425 BC) in the Luxor Museum, Egypt. The original is carved in greywacke – a silicate rock made up of fine clay particles embedded with varying proportions of coarser sand grains. This pharaoh, famous for his conquests of neighbouring lands, is not only sporting a very natty line in the aforementioned 'chin wig', but is also adorned in the striped headcloth so typical of the pharaohs.

The *nemes*, famously depicted on the gold face mask of Tutankhamun, is a striped cloth pulled tight across the forehead, spreading sideways over the shoulders and down over the back of the head. On the sides, two 'lappets' hang down over the front of the shoulders. The nemes and the false beard together define this bust as an Egyptian pharaoh as clearly as if it were written across the front.

On the top of the head is the Ureaus – a cobra, curled and ready to strike – that was a symbol of kingship. The cobra-goddess Wadjyt was a very early cult symbol of Lower Egypt and was included in the pharaoh's royal regalia as a protective symbol associated with the sun-god Ra, and as a symbol of his rule over Upper and Lower Egypt. The cobra's head is vulnerable to being broken off (as it is in the original statue and in many other examples), so I have kept it closer to the head than the original may have been.

If the carving, with its horizontal stripes and the boldly defined features of the face, has a slightly Art Deco look about it, that is no coincidence. Egyptian style, highlighted by the excavation of Tutankhamun's tomb in 1922, was a major influence on the Art Deco style of the 1920s and 30s.

TOOLS
1½lb (655g) dummy mallet • 2½lb (1175g) club hammer • marble point/punch • ¾in (20mm) claw chisel • 2in (50mm) bolster/pitcher • ³⁄₁₆in (4mm) chisel • ¼in (6mm) chisel • ½in (13mm) chisel • ¾in (20mm) chisel • ¼in (6mm) gouge • ½in (13mm) gouge • ¾in (20mm) gouge • stone rasp

MATERIALS
Limestone block 15 x 9in (380 x 230mm) and 15in (380mm) high
Weight approx. 175lb (80kg) – use lifting gear

Scale drawing on a 1in (25mm) grid. Enlarge drawing to the required size (see page 10).

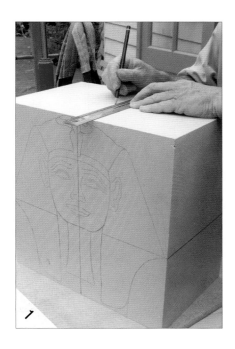

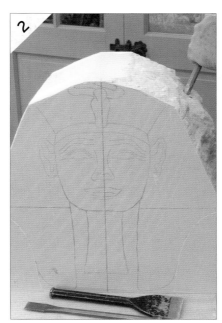

PREPARATIONS

1 Get a block of limestone 15 x 9in (380 x 230mm) and 15in (380mm) high. **Weight warning: this will weigh about 175lb (80kg), so use lifting gear.** Make a full-size copy of the drawing and trace the front pattern onto the front of the block. Also trace the outline onto the back of the block, making sure it lines up with the front. Draw a centreline up the front and back and across the top.

ROUGHING OUT

2 Cut away the surplus stone at the sides using point, claw and bolster. Work up to the tracing lines of the nemes headcloth on the front and back. Dress the surface with the bolster to get it flat and reasonably smooth. This surface will form the edge of the carving in due course, and you need it flat for the next step.

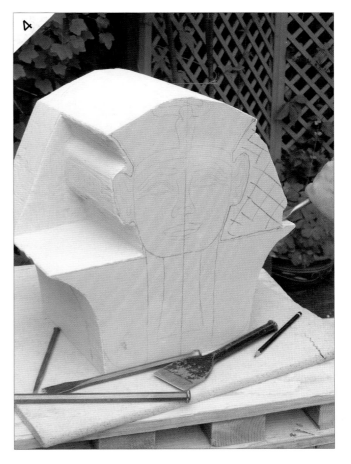

3 Lay the stone sideways on the surface you have just flattened so you can cut away the surplus stone around the shoulders, working up to the lappets of the headcloth. The stone is heavy and difficult to manoeuvre on the banker, so take care not to hurt yourself and get someone to help you if necessary. The shoulders are cut away, as is often done with a bust, to provide a smaller base for the head.

4 Mark the line of the outer edges of the headcloth by measuring 5½in (140mm) back from the front edge. Cut out the surplus stone between these edges and the sides of the face, leaving the ears untouched for now. Don't cut too close to the face at this stage. Make sure both sides are balanced.

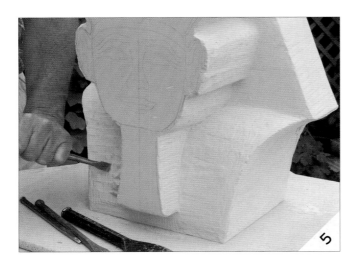

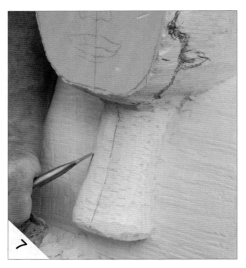

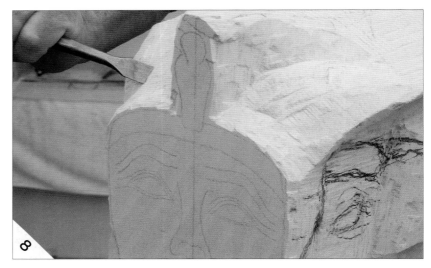

5 Draw a smooth curve for the shoulders, starting 1½in (40mm) back from the bottom front edge and curving up to the headcloth ends, then back down to the back. Chisel away the stone around and under the beard and the sides of the face to shape the lappets up to where they join the headcloth. Take care not to damage the acute angles of the upper edges.

6 Cut away the stone from the ears back to about 4in (100mm) from the front edge, and slope them back towards the headcloth. They will be cut back further later.

CARVING THE FACE

7 Draw the side profile onto the head by referring to the drawing and the tracing on the front. Mark the levels of the nose, lips, eyes and headband from the front tracing to the sides, then measure the distance of each of the elements from the front edge using the drawing. This is for guidance only; you will not cut right back to these lines, but they will help you visualize the face as you carve. Start by carving the beard so the top is about 1¼in (30mm) back from the front edge. We will just leave it roughed out at this stage.

8 Remove some of the surplus stone at the top of the head to help you visualize the shape of the face as you work on it in the following steps. Leave the stone for the cobra untouched at this stage.

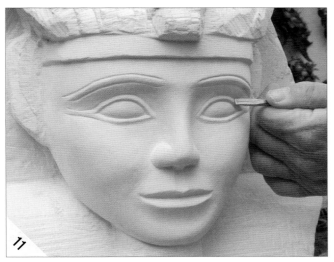

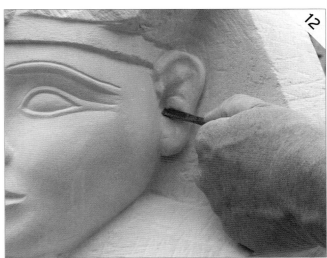

9 Forming the shape of the face is probably the hardest part of the job, and there are no simple steps to make it easier. Just take it steadily, a bit at a time, and don't remove stone you may need later. Hollow out the eyes first, then, starting from the tip of the nose where it is shown on the front tracing, work backwards and outwards to form the shape of the front of the face. Every element is further back than the nose, sometimes by a significant amount. I have left the stone for the cobra untouched so you can see how far back the forehead is. The chin goes back to where it meets the beard, and the sides of the face slope in towards the chin. The eyes have a tendency to creep downwards as you work, so keep checking their height against the drawing.

10 Go over the face carefully with the rasp to refine the features before moving on to the detail. If you look at people's faces (discreetly – don't stare!) you will see how there are grooves and hollows around the mouth, eyes and nose. Refine the shape of the jawline and join the chin neatly with the false beard.

11 Now carve in the detail of the lips, nostrils, eyelids, eyes, and the distinctive stylized eyebrows. This is easier than you might expect once you have created the shape of the face. But there is a pitfall: the slightest deviation in a feature, especially the mouth, will completely change the expression. Always draw in a feature before you carve it so you can see the effect it will have. Use the sharp corner of a small chisel to cut in the eyelids. Use fine abrasives to refine the finish as you complete each feature (the Egyptian original is very smooth).

12 To finish the face, carve the ears and refine the jawline. Adjust the headcloth as necessary to bring the forehead strap around the sides over the top of the ears. To carve ears you need to use a ¼in (6mm) gouge to create the curling flow of the ridges and hollows. Look at real ears to see how they are formed. Every pair is different, but there is a general pattern.

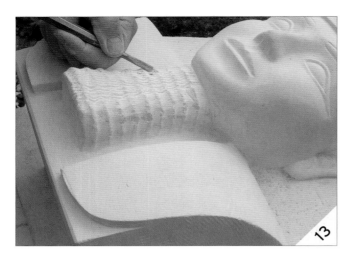

CARVING THE OTHER FEATURES

13 Mark out the edges of the lappets as shown on the drawing, and cut out the channel between them and the beard to a depth of about ⅜in (10mm). Lay the carving on its back and cut round the bottom of the lappets and beard to form the front edge of the base (put a chamfer along the edge). Carve the beard first by cutting grooves across it horizontally with a ½in (13mm) gouge, then use the point of a small chisel to carve wiggly lines up the beard, turning left onto the ridges and right into the hollows to create a hair texture. Remember that this is a stylized false beard, so don't aim for naturalism.

14 The lappets have narrow horizontal ridges about ¼in (6mm) wide. First draw parallel lines with a ruler about 1in (25mm) apart, using the base board as your datum – these will help you keep the lines level. To keep the cut lines parallel, use the concave side of a ¼in (6mm) gouge and push it across the

lappet, keeping it straight. Repeat the process with one point of the gouge in the last score line, like furrows in a field, checking the alignment with the pencil lines. Finish by scoring each cut deeper with the point of a small chisel.

15 Now we can finish shaping the head. Cut round the stone that will form the cobra, and use chisels and a rasp to shape the headcloth over the top of the head. Note how the cloth and headband are shaped at the sides. Use the claw to remove the surplus rock at the back so that there is a steady curve over the back of the head and from the centreline to both edges of the headcloth. Keep a smooth curve at the edge of the shoulders.

16 Mark out and carve the cobra, with its head rearing up and leaning back, and its body curling up to the top of the head. Make sure you leave enough stone to support the head. Undercut round the body to make it look detached.

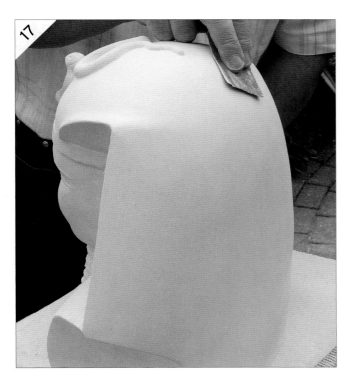

17 Use the rasp and 120-grit abrasive to bring the headcloth to a smooth finish (this will be the surface of the wider stripes). At the bottom of the back, shape the baseline to a curve and put a chamfer on the edge.

18 Now mark out the stripes, with horizontal lines on the front side panels that turn sharply round the sides and curve down the back. The lines from the top of the head flow straight over to intersect with the lines on the back. Between each wider stripe of ⅝in (15mm) there is a ½in (13mm) stripe that is cut to a depth of about ¹⁄₁₆in (2mm).

THE FINISHED PIECE

19 Wash off all the dust. Thutmose III is now ready to face the world again after 3,500 years. Use these photos as a reference when you are carving the detail.

GOTHIC GRIFFON

You would think there were enough real creatures in the world to satisfy the creative instincts of carvers, but for thousands of years humankind has been inventing mythical beasts combining the features of two or more mammals, reptiles, birds and fishes. This 'mix and match' approach goes back at least to Ancient Egypt (sphinxes) and Ancient Greece (centaurs, minotaurs and many others).

But the prize for inventing the most exciting and scariest creatures must go to the Gothic carvers of the Middle Ages. There seemed to be no limit to the inter-species combinations they could dream up.

The griffon, griffin or gryphon is a mythical beast with the head and wings of an eagle and the body of a lion. Either creature would be frightening on its own, but a giant flying lion–eagle hybrid dropping out of the sky to tear you apart with its beak and claws would have given many a medieval child sleepless nights. And that scare appeal still thrills today in the many 'witches and wizards' fantasies such as the *Harry Potter* stories.

The most usual forms for Gothic stone carvings of mythical beasts were as 'supporters' on heraldic shields or as gargoyles peering (or leering) down from churches and cathedrals. It is said that medieval masons chose to make gargoyles frightening to keep the Devil out of the church, but given the subject matter of some of them it is hard to escape the conclusion they were just having a bit of fun. As well as scary beasts, they often used grotesque quasi-human forms in poses that were comical, irreverent or even downright rude.

A functioning gargoyle would not make a good hobby carving project: it has a large block of stone at the back end, where it is built into the wall, and it has to be hollowed like a drainpipe to channel rainwater off a roof and project it (out of its mouth) away from the foundations of the building. I have instead based this project loosely on a 15th-century carved wooden pew end illustrated in *Pugin's Gothic Ornament*. This griffon is lying down ('*couchant*' in heraldic terms), making it more compact and therefore more economical in the quantity of stone required. Instead of the downward-looking pose of a gargoyle, it can lurk in the shrubbery like an escaped supporter from a heraldic shield, ready to pounce on the unwary.

TOOLS

1½lb (655g) dummy mallet ● 2½lb (1175g) club hammer ● marble point/punch ● ¾in (20mm) claw chisel ● 2in (50mm) bolster/pitcher ● ³⁄₁₆in (4mm) chisel ● ¼in (6mm) chisel ● ½in (13mm) chisel ● ¾in (20mm) chisel ● ¼in (6mm) gouge ● ½in (13mm) gouge ● ¾in (20mm) gouge ● stone rasp ● stone/concrete saw

MATERIALS

Limestone block 18 x 9in (460 x 230mm) and 12in (300mm) high

Weight approx. 170lb (77kg) – use lifting gear

Scale drawing on a 1in (25mm) grid. Enlarge drawing to the required size (see page 10).

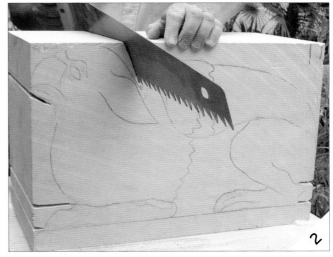

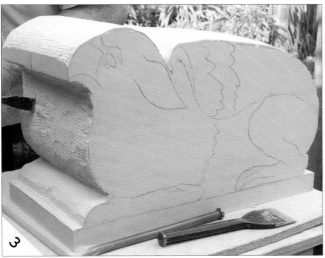

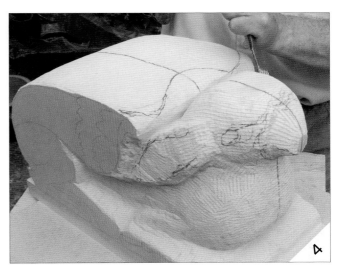

PREPARATIONS

1 Get a block of limestone 18 x 9in (460 x 230mm) and 12in (300mm) high. **Weight warning: this will weigh about 170lb (77kg), so use lifting gear.** Make a full-size copy of the drawing and trace the side profile onto both sides of the block. Scratch in the outlines so you don't lose them as you work.

2 It is best to start by making some 'relieving' cuts with the saw (or angle grinder if you are careful and don't mind the dust). Cut into the deepest parts of the outline between the head and wings, around the feet and base, under the rump and, very carefully, under the beak. These cuts make it much easier to excavate these areas and define some key points in the boundaries of the pattern.

ROUGHING OUT

3 Remove the surplus stone outside the side profile, taking care not to damage the piece that will be the beak. Cut straight across from the tracing lines on each side using point, claw and bolster. You don't need a perfect surface as it will all be carved later, but try to get it reasonably level as it will help you to position the elements correctly later.

4 Draw a centreline up both ends and along the top of the stone, and draw the outline of the head, ears, wings and back end, using the plan drawing as your guide. Rough out the sides of the body from the tip of the beak back to the rear haunches, leaving the wings, legs and rear haunches untouched for now. The body width across the chest should be about 6in (150mm) overall at this stage. Leave plenty of stone for the ears and facial features.

155

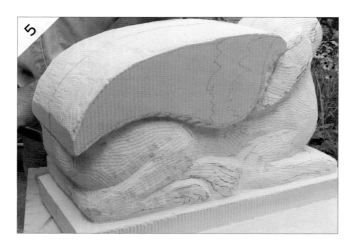

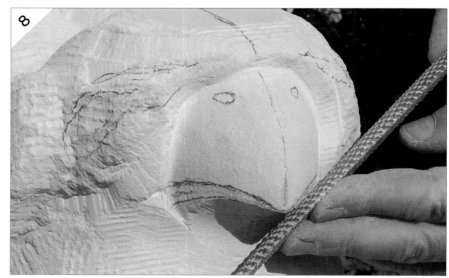

5 Now shape the rump and haunches (the lion part) under the wings. Cut under the wing edges and carefully make a ½in (13mm) saw cut along the top edge of the base. Cut the legs and feet back to this line. Leave some stone for the tail under the rear end and up behind the right leg (or left if you prefer).

6 Finish the roughing out by shaping the wings. Cut a large V down the back, and round the wings over from the middle of the back to their outer edges. At the back end of the wings, bring the feathers almost to a point that sits a little out from the rump and haunches.

DETAIL CARVING: THE BASE

7 It is best to work on the base now while the piece can still be laid on its side. The Gothic style favours large round mouldings, so I have given the base a thick semicircular bull-nose moulding with rounded corners. Draw lines along the top and bottom faces ½in (13mm) in from the edge. Make two semicircular card templates with diameters of 1⅜in (34mm) and ⅞in (23mm). Use these to mark the inner and outer lines for the rounded corners. Shape the corners to the larger diameter using the rasp, then round over the entire length of the moulding back to the guidelines.

CARVING THE HEAD

8 Start the head by shaping the beak. Measure from the drawing to mark the positions of the tip of the beak, the top point and the width of the sides. Chisel away the surplus stone, then refine the shape with the rasp. Draw on the centreline as a reference point, and draw in the mouth.

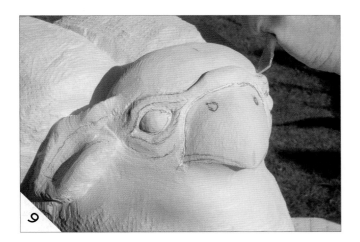

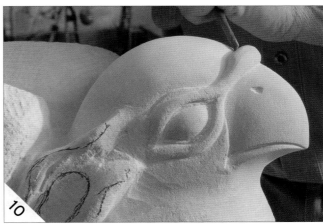

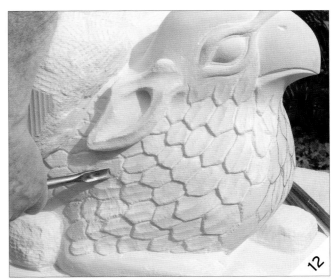

9 Remove more surplus stone to fix the positions of the eyes, the ears and the large lump at the top of the beak (called the *cere* in ornithological terms). Shape the dome of the head and cut away stone around and under the ears to refine the shape of the face. Note how the head is tilted back with the cere at the highest point of the carving.

10 Now carve in the fine detail of the eyes and eyelids, the mouth, the nostrils (which would be in the cere in a real eagle), the 'eyebrows' and the cere. Give plenty of definition to the features and make it look suitably menacing – griffons are not sweet-natured.

11 Carve the detail of the ears, which are large, pointed and more like a demon rabbit's than anything a lion or eagle might possess. Shape the neck to the correct width around the ears, and shape the back of the ears into the head.

CARVING THE OTHER 'EAGLE' PARTS

12 The front end of the griffon is covered in feathers. Refine the shape of the body with chisels and rasp first so you are not putting feathers on a bad shape. Refine the shape of the front legs a little more, as the feathers lay over them slightly at the elbows. Draw the outline of all the feathers, with the lines flowing from under the beak and eyes and out to the edges. Use a small chisel to outline the feather edges, and carve two grooves up each feather with a ½in (13mm) gouge. Create bold shadows at the edges.

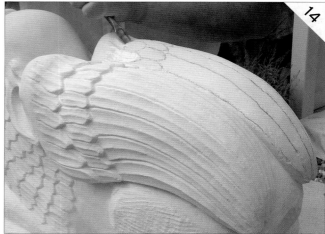

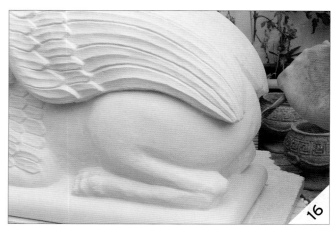

13 Refine the shape of the wings by creating a dip behind the leading edges and a shallow groove down the centre. Deeply undercut the leading edge. Bring the wings to a point at the rump end.

14 Carve the wing feathers similar to the breast, but make them bigger and bolder. Curl the forward feathers out at the ends so they are clearly separated from the long flight feathers. Give plenty of definition to the flight feathers.

CARVING THE 'LION' PARTS

15 We now switch from eagle to lion features, starting with the front feet and the tail. Carve three grooves across the feet from side to side behind the knuckle joints of the toes and ankle, giving them a slight curve to reflect the splay of the toes. Carve grooves lengthways to separate the foot into four toes (with a little 'thumb' claw a bit further back on the inside). Shape the rather knobbly toes and their pointed claws. Use a gouge to carve grooves along the leg back to the elbow to give it a sinewy look. Shape the tail on the left side, coming out under the leg and dividing into waves, curls and hairs at the end.

16 Refine the shape of the rump so it curves smoothly round to the sides into the haunches. Try to make the haunches look muscular and energetic. Carve the rear feet similar to the front, and give the legs the same sinewy look from the toes back to the elbow at the back. Undercut the feet so they appear detached from the base.

THE FINISHED PIECE

17 Wash off the dust. The griffon is now finished and ready to frighten children. Use these photos as a reference when you are carving the detail.

REPAIRING STONE CARVINGS

The best way to deal with damage is to prevent it from happening, but if the worst happens and you break a piece off a stone carving, either during carving or later, all is not lost – you can effect an almost-invisible repair.

Clean breaks can be glued back together using diluted PVA adhesive. Larger cracks and holes can be filled with a limestone mixture. Save the limestone powder you create when using the rasp or saw and keep it in a jar. You can use this as a filler by mixing it with builders' lime (3 parts stone dust to 1 part lime) or with diluted PVA adhesive.

DOLPHIN PEDESTAL

There is one mammal that features more than any other in Classical decoration: the dolphin. However, our ancestors were not as anatomically aware as us and did not recognize dolphins as mammals. Dolphins swam in the sea, and therefore were thought of as fish. When they portrayed dolphins, they endowed them with the features of fish – gills, scales and spiky fins – even though these features were noticeably absent from the smooth-skinned, air-breathing creatures.

To be fair, most of the artists and carvers of the non-coastal parts of Europe had probably never seen a real dolphin. They simply embellished earlier portrayals with ever more exaggerated fishy features until the resemblance to the actual creature became increasingly remote.

In this project, I have kept to the Classical tradition with two very fishy dolphins supporting a pedestal in the typical 'heads down, tails up' posture, further embellished by the 'intertwined bodies' variant. This variant works well in a two-dolphin pedestal; a similar pose is used to excellent effect on the cast-iron lamp columns around Westminster Bridge in London, UK.

As this is the last project in the book, and you will be sourcing and adapting your own designs after this, I would like you to give particular thought to the design issues I had to resolve in this project. They may not be immediately obvious, but every part of the design had to be considered on the basis of aesthetics and practicality, and this is how you will have to approach your own designs.

For aesthetic purposes, the dolphins need to look light and lively, but this has to be balanced by practical considerations and providing a sound structure that will endure many years of use outdoors. Will the base break off at the corners? Will the neck of the pedestal survive a heavy urn placed off-balance? How should we portray the parts of the pedestal that are not dolphin? If you look closely at the piece, you will see how I have resolved all these issues.

This pedestal can be used on its own to support a vase or flower urn, but it will look best with the shell dish in project 14. If you combine the two, you will have a Classical garden ornament that will mark the completion of your journey through this book and bring you many years of pleasure.

TOOLS
1½lb (655g) dummy mallet • 2½lb (1175g) club hammer • marble point/punch • ¾in (20mm) claw chisel • 2in (50mm) bolster/pitcher • ³⁄₁₆in (4mm) chisel • ¼in (6mm) chisel • ½in (13mm) chisel • ¾in (20mm) chisel • ¼in (6mm) gouge • ½in (13mm) gouge • ¾in (20mm) gouge • stone rasp

MATERIALS
Limestone block 15 x 9in (380 x 230mm) and 15in (380mm) high
Weight approx. 175lb (80kg) – use lifting gear

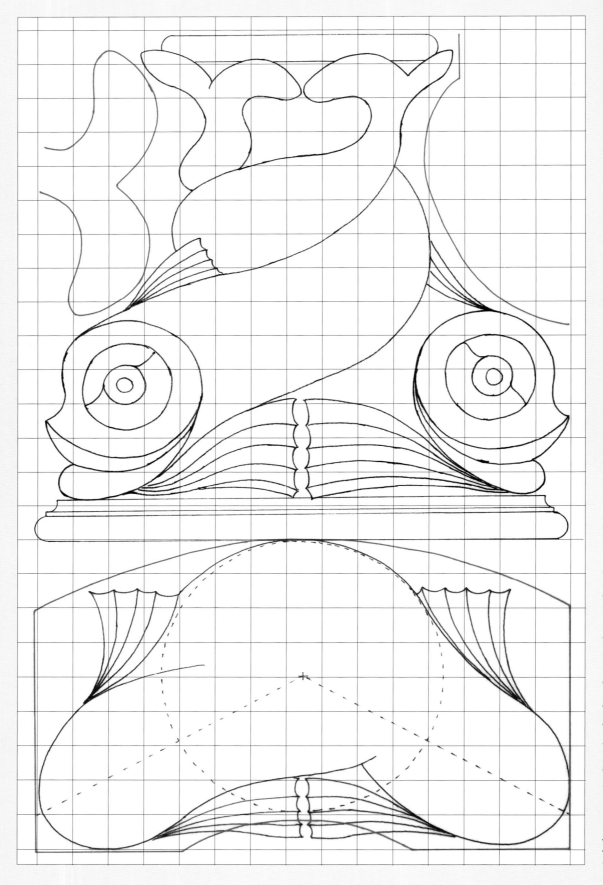

Scale drawing on a 1in (25mm) grid. Enlarge drawing to the required size (see page 10).

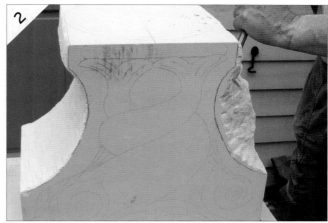

PREPARATIONS

1 Get a block of limestone 15 x 9in (380 x 230mm) and 15in (380mm) high. **Weight warning: this will weigh about 175lb (80kg), so use lifting gear.** Make a full-size copy of the drawing and trace the dolphin pattern onto the front (this helps to envisage the shape at the start). Use a template of the curved green line on the drawing to mark the cut-away areas at the sides. Draw an 8in (200mm) diameter circle on the top, with its centre 1in (25mm) back from the centre point of the block. Also draw a 9in (230mm) incomplete circle on the same centre.

ROUGHING OUT

2 Start by cutting away the areas at the sides that you marked with the template. You don't need to work it to a good finish; it is just a way to help you balance up the carving at the beginning.

3 Rough out around the outside of the 9in (230mm) circle, leaving a depth of around 1½in (40mm) before cutting under to round off the top part of the pedestal. The back edge remains vertical at this stage, and the front edge is not cut in as deep as the sides.

4 On each side, draw a vertical line 1in (25mm) back from the front edge, and continue this across the roughed-out surface towards the centre point of the top circle. This line gives you the orientation of the dolphins' heads. Roughly draw in the spiral of the dolphins' bodies and the position of the dorsal fins. Now remove surplus stone at the back, and start to roughly shape the dolphins' heads and bodies, leaving plenty of spare stone at this stage.

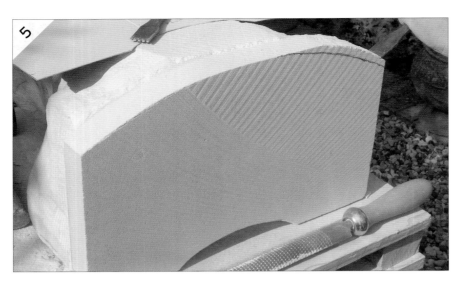

SHAPING THE BASE AND TOP

5 Lay the piece down to get at the underside. Make a template of the underside profile as shown on the plan, and mark this on the base, making sure it is the right way round (with the long curve at the back). Cut carefully and accurately round the profile to get a good vertical edge for the base moulding, which we will finish later. Standing the carving on a cork mat helps to protect the edges and corners from damage while you work..

6 Draw the dolphin tails around the top circle, with the V of each tail directly above the dolphin's head. Use the tail template shown in green on the drawing. Cut round the edge of the 8in (200mm) circle, leaving the dolphin tails standing out.

SHAPING THE DOLPHINS

7 By referring to the drawing and the finished photos, redraw the details on the dolphins' heads. Form the shape of the heads and fins, but leave the detail to be carved later. Check the measurements on each side to make sure all the features are in the same position on both sides of both heads. The head has a pronounced domed forehead, which is about as close as we get to a real dolphin. Use a rasp to get a smooth rounded surface around the lips and the dome of the head.

8 Now chisel out the spiral of the bodies from the tails down to their respective heads. The dolphin on your left is always one level higher than the one on your right. Feel your way a little at a time, as you can't put stone back once you have removed it. Form the dorsal fin just behind the head, touching the body of the other dolphin to reduce the risk of breaking. Excavate the pedestal a little under the tail fins – this will be refined later.

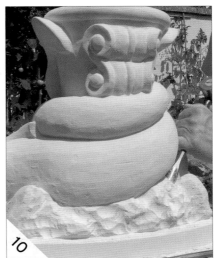

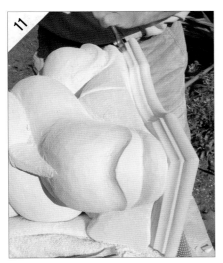

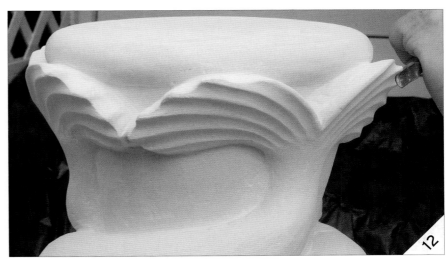

CARVING THE TOP, BACK AND BASE

9 Form the shape of the tails so they curl under the top of the pedestal and out again. Shape the pedestal in between the tails to a thickness of about 6in (150mm) when you are 3in (75mm) below the top. Carefully form a ¾in (20mm) *torus* moulding to finish the top of the pedestal. There is a large gap between the tails at the back of the pedestal, so to embellish it and give invisible support to the structure, add an S-shaped volute scroll across the back.

10 There is another large dolphin-less gap at the back under the lowest dolphin. To fill this, we shape the surplus stone into rugged rocks as though the dolphin were lying on a sea-washed rocky outcrop. This is best done with a ¾in (20mm) gouge. Sculpt deep channels, hollows and knobbly bits to make it look as natural as possible.

11 Lay the carving onto its side on a soft surface to protect the tail fins. Carve out a rebate ¾in (20mm) up from the bottom edge and ¼in (6mm) in from the outer edge. Shape the resulting projection into a ¾in (20mm) *torus* moulding using a large gouge and the rasp. Measure ¼in (6mm) in from the new edge and carve a ⅜in (10mm) *cavetto* moulding using a medium gouge and an ordinary round file. Make sure the mouldings are straight and level, with clean mitres at the corners.

CARVING THE DETAIL ON THE DOLPHINS

12 Carve the 'fishy' spikes and curves on the tail fins, making sure they flow naturally and gracefully into the body. Shape the top edges into the top of the pedestal. Don't make the spiky points too sharp or they will break off in use.

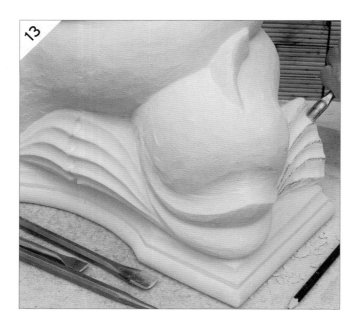

13 Shape the side fins, starting just behind the mouth and sprouting up and outwards. Make them symmetrical, with the front set slightly overhanging the base and meeting at the centre of the carving.

14 Carefully draw in the features of the face to make sure everything looks right and is symmetrical and at the right level before you start chiselling. Make it a rule always to draw a feature before you cut it. Start by carving a hollow under the eyes, and an eyelid over the eye to leave the eyeball standing out. Cut a V around the large circles that spring from the jawline and around the eye.

15 Shape the eyeball into a 1in (25mm) dome, and cut a ¼in (6mm) hollow in the middle to represent the pupil. Carefully shape the eyelid and the area under the eye. Use a large gouge to continue the hollow above the upper lip all the way around the head in a circle, to represent gills. As it comes back over the top of the head at the front, the hollow separates into two grooves. Try to create bold distinctive features that are symmetrical on both sides of the carving.

16 Carve the dorsal fins on each dolphin's back, just behind the head. Note how the fins are 'pressed' into a curve where they touch the body of the other dolphin.

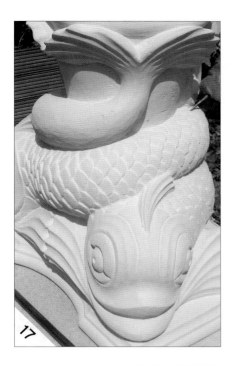

17 Mark the scales carefully in regular alternating curves following the twist of the body, starting about 1in (25mm) across and getting gradually smaller as the body gets thinner. Carve all the scales as neatly as possible using a ¼in (6mm) chisel to cut round the back edge of each scale, then a ½in (13mm) chisel to hollow it slightly towards the head end, creating an apparent overlap from front to back and bottom to top. There are a lot of scales (about 500 of them) and they will look a mess if you are not neat and careful, so take your time and get it right.

THE FINISHED PIECE

18 Now at last the job is finished. Wash off all the dust and tidy up any uneven carving exposed by the washing. These photos illustrate how the piece should look from the front, back and sides – use them as a reference when you are carving the detail.

19 If you have made the shell dish (project 14), you can now set up the complete ensemble and spend many happy hours enjoying the fruits of your labours.

GLOSSARY OF STYLISTIC, ARCHITECTURAL AND STONEMASONRY TERMS

Acanthus

A plant with large indented leaves and tall flower spikes. Used abundantly in stylized form in Classical decoration. **1**, **2**

Arris (pl.: arrisses)

The distinct square edges along a worked block of stone or a moulding. A sharp unchipped arris is a sign of quality in craftsmanship. A softener on the banker, such as a cork mat, helps to protect the arris from being damaged by resting on chips of stone.

Art Deco

A style of design popular in the 1920s and 30s characterized by bold geometrical lines and bold but limited colours such as black, white, silver and gold.

Art Nouveau

A late Victorian and Edwardian style of design popular from around 1890 to 1914, characterized mainly by stylized plants and flowers, particularly associated with fin-de-siecle Paris. Known as *Jugendstil* in Germany and Eastern Europe. (See page 35.)

Ashlar

A type of wall surface consisting of smooth-faced finely worked blocks of stone with straight square edges (arrisses) and narrow mortar joints. The most expensive of wall types, used for facing prestigious buildings. **3**

Baroque

A style of design that dominated Europe from around 1630 (starting in Italy) to around 1720. An exuberant form of the Roman Classical style, it is characterized by depth and richness of carved and painted decoration. (See page 34.)

Bedding plane

The way a stone is aligned to its 'natural bed' (see page 23). It may be natural-bedded (horizontal), tooth- or edge-bedded (vertical, end-on) or face-bedded (vertical, side-on).

Boss

A rounded stone, usually carved with foliage, at the junction of several ribs in a Gothic vaulted ceiling. Technically, it is a voussoir (see page 171) acting as a keystone in the arch of the ribbed vault. (See project 8.)

Capital

The distinctive decorated stone at the head of a column or pilaster. Capitals are a key component in defining the architectural style of a building. (See Classical styles right.) **4** *Classical Ionic,* **5** *Victorian Gothic*

Cartouche

A convex oval panel, framed usually with volutes, swirls and acanthus, frequently bearing a 'coat of arms'. Much used in Classical decoration, especially in the Baroque style. **6**

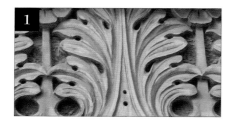

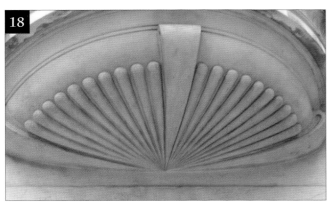

Classical styles

The term 'Classical' is applied to the decorative styles of Ancient Greece and Rome, and the later revivals of these styles from the 16th to 19th centuries. The purer Classical styles are divided into 'orders' – Tuscan, Doric, Ionic, Corinthian and Composite – defined mainly by the capitals of their columns, although there is considerable variation within each type. (See page 33.) **7** *Tuscan,* **8** *Doric,* **9** *Ionic,* **10** *Corinthian,* **11** *composite*

Corbel

A projection from a wall supporting a beam, arch or shelf. The Classical corbel, usually decorated with volutes and acanthus decoration, is used widely in Classical and Neoclassical architecture. Gothic corbels, usually decorated with plant forms, are used widely at the bases of vault ribs. **12** *Classical,* **13** *Gothic*

Crockets

A feature of Gothic buildings, comprising leaf-like projections up the corners of a gable or pinnacle. (See project 7.) **14**

Finial

A decorative feature at the top of a wall, steeple, gate pier, vase or any other vertical feature to give definition to the uppermost point. (See project 12.) **15**

Flying buttress

A buttress is a projection on the side or corner of a wall designed to prevent the wall being pushed sideways by the weight of the roof. A flying buttress is a Gothic refinement in which the sideways force is projected further out over to the aisle wall of a church to give greater resistance to the outward force of the ceiling vault and allow bigger windows in the clerestory above the nave. **16**

Frieze

A decorative pattern along a horizontal feature such as a string-course, entablature or the base of a column. (See projects 4, 5 and 6.) **17**

Gadroon

A raised repeating pattern of beads (in a straight pattern) or 'teardrops' (in a curved pattern) commonly used on vases and around the edges of furniture and dishes. **18**

Gargoyle

A defining feature of medieval Gothic churches. Their primary purpose is as a water-spout to conduct rainwater from a roof and project it away from the building, but gargoyles were traditionally carved in grotesque human or animal form. (See project 17.) **19**

Gothic

One of the key styles in the history of stone carving, associated mainly with medieval churches and cathedrals from around 1150 to 1500, and later with the Victorian Gothic Revival from around 1830 to 1900. Key features are tracery windows, ribbed vaults, gargoyles, crockets, flying buttresses and pointed arches.

Heraldry

The identification of an individual or corporation by a 'coat of arms' consisting of devices on a shield, usually accompanied by a crest on top of a helm above the shield and 'supporters' (animal or human) either side of the shield, and a motto. A key component of carved and painted decoration from the 12th century to the present day. **20**

Niche

A recess in a wall, usually concave, often for displaying statues. In Classical styles it is often topped with an inverted shell. **21**

Pilaster

A pilaster is similar to a column but is attached to the wall and is usually flat. Classical pilasters have the same bases and capitals as columns and are often used on the wall side of a colonnade. **22**

Pinnacle

Similar to a finial, but more pyramidal in shape. Much used on Gothic buildings, usually encrusted with crockets. **23**

Polychromatic decoration

The use of colour to decorate stone carvings, much used in the Middle Ages. Carved mouldings and statues of saints were often brightly painted, unlike their present appearance.

Quatrefoil

A decorative element much used in Gothic decoration, shaped like a four-leaf clover. Also common are trefoils (three leaves) and cinquefoils (five leaves). **24**

Renaissance

The 'rebirth' of Greek and Roman Classical decoration that started in Italy in the 15th century and spread across Europe to become firmly established by the early 17th century. (See page 35.)

Rococo

The most exuberant of the 18th-century decorative styles, characterized by elaborate gilded swirls and pastel-coloured paintwork. It is the style most associated with the palaces of Europe and Western Russia, and later with the 'fun palaces' of the late 19th century: theatres, ballrooms and music halls. **25**

Spandrel

The roughly triangular area between an arch and the rectangle surrounding it. Spandrels are frequently carved with plant patterns that project into the corners. **26**

String-course

A horizontal band of stones along an external wall, usually at the floor/ceiling level of each floor. It usually projects outwards with a 'weathering' at the top to throw off water, and a curved moulding underneath often carved with decoration. (See project 6.) **27**

Swag/festoon

A decoration, usually depicting flowers, fruit, fabric, birds or game, suspended by one or both ends and 'draped' around a panel, vase or other feature. Much used in Classical decoration. **28**

Template (templet)

A flat piece of board, card, metal or plastic cut to the exact shape and size of a face or profile of a block of stone for the purpose of shaping the stone precisely. Masons have used templates since ancient times to ensure that each stone in a building (and especially an arch, dome or vault) fits exactly into place when installed.

Tracery

A fine filigree of stone that forms the framework for a Gothic window or screen. It consists of mullions, transoms, interconnecting pointed arches and ancillary features such as cusps, eyes and foils. **29**

Vault

A stone ceiling set in what is in effect a continuous arch. Its simplest form is the 'barrel' vault used in Classical and Romanesque architecture. Medieval Gothic architecture took vault-making to its zenith by combining the pointed arch with tracery to produce the magnificent fan and lierne vaults, with their slender ribs and decorated bosses, which are the glory of medieval cathedrals. (See project 8.) **30**

Volute

A spiral curl used abundantly in Classical decoration, mainly as a single curl on capitals and an S-shaped double volute on the sides of corbels and other supports. **31**

Voussoirs

The segments that make up an arch. They may be regular wedge-shaped segments of a circle in a Classical arch, or they may be variable in shape in Gothic and other complex arches. The uppermost voussoir is known as a keystone (or a boss in a ribbed vault), but each voussoir is of equal importance to the structure. **32**

COMMON MOULDINGS

Classical/general

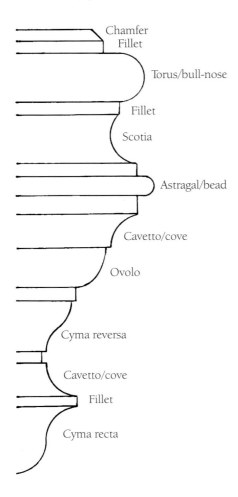

Chamfer
Fillet
Torus/bull-nose
Fillet
Scotia
Astragal/bead
Cavetto/cove
Ovolo
Cyma reversa
Cavetto/cove
Fillet
Cyma recta

Gothic

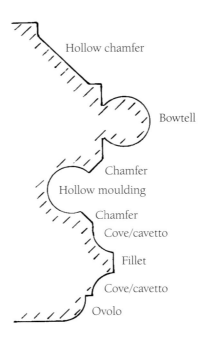

Hollow chamfer
Bowtell
Chamfer
Hollow moulding
Chamfer
Cove/cavetto
Fillet
Cove/cavetto
Ovolo

Linear moulding patterns

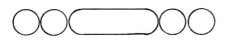

Bead & billet (usually on astragal)

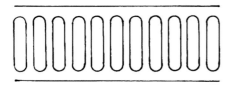

Fluted (concave on flat background)

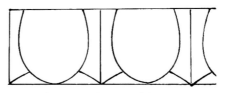

Egg & dart (usually on ovolo)

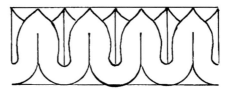

Waterleaf (usually on cyma recta)

ABOUT THE AUTHOR

Steve Bisco is well known to readers of *Woodcarving* magazine for his articles on period decorative woodcarving projects. He is the author of the woodcarving book, *Twenty Decorative Carving Projects in Period Styles*. He has been carving as a hobby for more than 25 years and is inspired by a love of historic buildings. His 'mission' has been to make traditional period styles of carving accessible to the average hobby carver in the average home.

Having more recently applied his carving experience to stone carving, Steve was surprised by an almost total lack of books on the subject and has set out on a new mission: to make traditional stone carving accessible to the domestic carver.

Steve grew up on an island near the ancient Roman town of Colchester, England, where he still lives with his wife Jenny. They have a daughter, Josephine, who lives near New York, and a son, Toby, who lives in London.

BIBLIOGRAPHY

Borromini, Anthony Blunt
Allen Lane/Penguin Books, 1979
ISBN 978-0-7139-1025-4 • www.penguin.co.uk

British Museum Dictionary of Ancient Egypt,
Ian Shaw and Paul Nicholson
The British Museum Press, 1995
ISBN 978-0-7141-1909-0 • www.britishmuseum.org

Carving Architectural Detail in Wood, Frederick Wilbur
Guild of Master Craftsman Publications, 2000
ISBN 978-1-86108-158-2 • www.gmcbooks.com

Carving Classical Styles in Wood, Frederick Wilbur
Guild of Master Craftsman Publications, 2004
ISBN 978-1-86108-363-0 • www.gmcbooks.com

Guided by a Stonemason, Thomas Maude
I.B. Tauris Publishers, 1997
ISBN 978-1-86064-039-1 • www.ibtauris.com

Handbook of Ornament, Franz Sales Meyer
Dover Publications, 1957
ISBN 978-0-48620-302-7 • www.doverpublications.com

Practical Stone Masonry, P.R. Hill & J.C.E. David
Donhead Publishing Ltd., 1995
ISBN 978-1-873394-14-4 • www.donhead.com

Pugin's Gothic Ornament, A.C. Pugin
Dover Publications, 1987
ISBN 978-0-48625-500-2 • www.doverpublications.com

The Parthenon Sculptures in the British Museum,
Ian Jenkins
The British Museum Press, 2007
ISBN 978-0-7141-2261-8 • www.britishmuseum.org

INDEX

To place an order, or to request a catalogue, contact:

GMC Publications, Castle Place, 166 High Street,
Lewes, East Sussex BN7 1XU United Kingdom
Tel: +44 (0)1273 488005 Fax: +44 (0)1273 402866
www.gmcbooks.com